CHOICES:
RESPONSIBLE DECISIONS
FOR A GODLY LIFE

CHOICES:
RESPONSIBLE DECISIONS FOR A GODLY LIFE

ROBERT F. KIRK

authorHOUSE®

AuthorHouse™
1663 Liberty Drive
Bloomington, IN 47403
www.authorhouse.com
Phone: 1-800-839-8640

Published by AuthorHouse 08/27/2015

ISBN: 978-1-4969-5982-9 (sc)
ISBN: 978-1-4969-5983-6 (hc)
ISBN: 978-1-4969-5981-2 (e)

Library of Congress Control Number: 2014922413

Print information available on the last page.

NLT
Scripture quotations marked NLT are taken from the Holy Bible, New Living Translation, copyright © 1996, 2004, 2007. Used by permission of Tyndale House Publishers, Inc. Carol Stream, Illinois 60188. All rights reserved. Website

NIV
Scripture quotations marked NIV are taken from the Holy Bible, New International Version®. NIV®. Copyright © 1973, 1978, 1984 by International Bible Society. Used by permission of Zondervan. All rights reserved. [Biblica]

CONTENTS

Dedication ix
Should I Read this Book? xi
Choices – An Introduction xv

Step 1: Choices – Reality and God 1
Step 2: Choices – Consequences 9
Step 3: Choices – Boundaries 11
Step 4: Choices – A Partnership with God 13
Step 5: Choices – Truth 19
Step 6: Choices – A Meaningful Life 23
Step 7: Choices – Wisdom 25

Personal Story 1 – Choosing Doors of Opportunity 33

Step 8: Choices – Thinking 43
Step 9: Choices – Becoming an Intelligent Person 45
Step 10: Choices – A Good Reputation 47
Step 11: Choices – Self-Control 49
Step 12: Choices – Riches 51
Step 13: Choices – Worry 53

**Personal Story 2 – Never Underestimate the Influence You
Have on Others! 55**

Step 14: Choices – Discretion 59
Step 15: Choices – Despising Advice 61
Step 16: Choices – Sin and Self-Control 63
Step 17: Choices – Integrity and Honesty 65
Step 18: Choices – Health 67
Step 19: Choices – Avoiding Life's Traps 71

Step 20: Choices – Fear and Protection 75
Step 21: Choices – Guidance for Our Lives 79
Step 22: Choices – Godliness 83
Step 23: Choices – Omniscient God...................................85
Step 24: Choices – Truth...87
Step 25: Choices – Honoring God......................................89
Step 26: Choices – Being Godly..91
Step 27: Choices – Hope 93
Step 28: Choices – Understanding Our Path......................95
Step 29: Choices – Planning for Parents and Children 97

      Financial Planning for Parents.....................................99
      Spiritual Planning for Parents.................................. 101

Step 30: Choices – Discipline... 103
Step 31: Choices – Trouble in Our Family........................109
Step 32: Choices – Children are Known by Their Acts 111
Step 33: Choices – Education and Instruction................. 115
Step 34: Choices – Long Life.. 119
Step 35: Choices – Avoiding Evil in the World 123
Step 36: Choices – Becoming a Fool 127
Step 37: Choices – Alcohol and Wine.............................. 131

Personal Story 3 – A Future Lost................................**133**

Step 38: Choices – Honesty.. 135

Personal Story 4 – Your Impact on Others **139**

Step 39: Choices – Laziness.. 143
Step 40: Choices – Don't Talk Too Much 147
Step 41: Choices – Harsh Words 151
Step 42: Choices – Anger 153
Step 43: Choices – Perverse Talk.................................... 155
Step 44: Choices – Helping the Poor............................... 157

Personal Story 5 – Helping the Poor..159

Step 45: Choices – Being Good to Others 163

Personal Story 6 – Failing Another..165

Step 46: Choices – Love 167
Step 47: Choices – Becoming Prosperous......................................171
Step 48: Choices – Haughtiness 173
Step 49: Choices – A Wife...175
Step 50: Choices – The Glory of Our Youth 177
Step 51: Choices – Working with the Unreliable............................179
Step 52: Choices – Bragging...181
Step 53: Choices – Going to War 183

Personal Story 7 – Vietnam Veterans..185

Step 54: Choices – Strength 187
Step 55: Choices – Friendship...189
Step 56: Choices – Guarding Your Heart 191
Step 57: Choices – Moral Leadership...193
Step 58: Choices – Happiness...195
Step 59: Choices – Immoral Women 197
Step 60: Choices – Summary 201

Statement of My Faith Concerning God's Salvation Message 205

References 207

DEDICATION

This book is dedicated to my wife Vicki. She is my best friend and my greatest helper and supporter. Without her assistance and support on this book it would not have been possible. I also want to thank God for his help and support in this book effort. I went to him constantly for guidance and wisdom in the writing of Choices. I give him all of the credit for any wisdom that may be found in Choices and I accept any and all errors.

This book is also dedicated to my grandchildren, their children, and their children's children.

A special dedication of this book is given to Sue Jones who waited years for its completion but left us before its publication. Sue, thank you for believing in me.

My thanks must go to Fran Savage who has been my authoring mentor. Her editing skills and author experience have been invaluable to me.
I want to give a special thanks to members of our small group Carol, Erin, Fran, Dick, Jeanne, Velda, Larry, and Edie who bravely took on the challenge to wade through early drafts of Choices. They made extremely valuable corrections, suggestions, and comments.

Lastly, I want to thank Niles and Tom who patiently listened over coffee as I fumbled and stuttered to try and pull ideas for the book out of my jumbled mind.

Should I Read this Book?

I always have a hard time deciding if I should purchase a particular book. In a bookstore I wander around picking up one book and then another. I look at the cover, read what others say about it and then check out the inside to see if I'll be interested in what the author has outlined. It's hard getting a good idea of what might be said in the book's pages. I guess the truth is I don't like the idea that I have to spend money to get the book in my hands just to start to read it and then decide it's not a book for me. I think, *I've wasted my money... maybe I can gift it.*

So, with this problem in mind, I have a developed a dichotomous key that will assist you in deciding if you would like to read this book. The following dichotomous key is a series of questions developed to aid you in your decision. If you respond "No" to any one of the key questions, then put the book down and go and find another that might better interest you. Isn't it great that I am trying to save you money?

Dichotomous Key

Should You Purchase This Book?

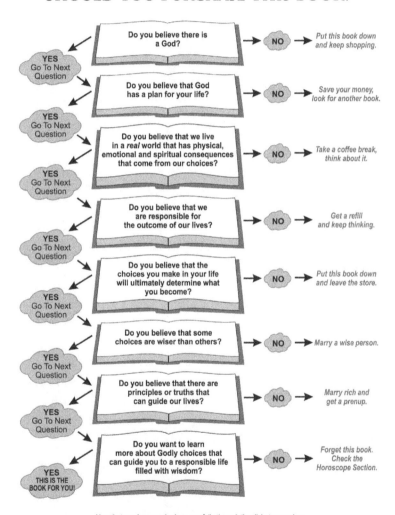

Do you believe there is a God?
NO → Put this book down and keep shopping.

YES Go To Next Question

Do you believe that God has a plan for your life?
NO → Save your money, look for another book.

YES Go To Next Question

Do you believe that we live in a *real* world that has physical, emotional and spiritual consequences that come from our choices?
NO → Take a coffee break, think about it.

YES Go To Next Question

Do you believe that we are responsible for the outcome of our lives?
NO → Get a refill and keep thinking.

YES Go To Next Question

Do you believe that the choices you make in your life will ultimately determine what you become?
NO → Put this book down and leave the store.

YES Go To Next Question

Do you believe that some choices are wiser than others?
NO → Marry a wise person.

YES Go To Next Question

Do you believe that there are principles or truths that can guide our lives?
NO → Marry rich and get a prenup.

YES Go To Next Question

Do you want to learn more about Godly choices that can guide you to a responsible life filled with wisdom?
NO → Forget this book. Check the Horoscope Section.

YES THIS IS THE BOOK FOR YOU!

Now that you have worked successfully through the dichotomous key you can safely purchase this book. Let's start learning about God, life and the important *Choices* of our lives.

CHOICES – AN INTRODUCTION

The author of the Biblical book of Proverbs was King Solomon. He had been chosen by God to be the next king of Israel after the death of his father, King David. At the time of becoming king he had a divine encounter with God. This encounter would change his world and our world forever.

God appeared to Solomon in a dream and asked him powerful questions followed by an amazing response from both Solomon and God.

> *That night God appeared to Solomon in a dream and said, "What do you want? Ask, and I will give it to you."*
> *Solomon replied to God, "You have been so faithful and kind to my father David, and now you have made me king in his place. Now Lord God, please keep your promise to David my father, for you have made me king*

over a people as numerous as the dust of the earth! Give me wisdom and knowledge to rule them properly, for who is able to govern this great nation of yours!"

God said to Solomon, "Because your greatest desire is to help your people, and you did not ask for personal wealth and honor or the death of your enemies or even a long life, but rather you asked for wisdom and knowledge to properly govern my people, I will certainly give you the wisdom and knowledge you requested. And I will also give you riches, wealth, and honor such as no other king has ever had before you or will ever have again!" 2 Chronicles 1: 7-12 (See also I Kings 3: 5-15)

Solomon began his reign as King of Israel with a set of great promises from God and for many years he was very successful in building up the power and influence of Israel. There were vast construction projects throughout the kingdom that demonstrated the power and wealth gained by Solomon's administration. His reputation spread throughout much of the known world as a King of great wealth and one of great wisdom. This is recorded in 2 Chronicles:

So King Solomon became richer and wiser than any other king in all the earth. Kings from every nation came to visit him and to hear the wisdom God had given him. 2 Chronicles 9: 22-23

It's his great wisdom that's recorded in the Books of Proverbs and in Ecclesiastes that has taken their rightful position as the wisdom literature in the Bible. It's from this wisdom that my book Choices is centered.

Solomon wrote hundreds, and perhaps thousands of Proverbs concerning various aspects of human life. These involved the use of Godly wisdom, wise observations, general principles, truths, practical matters, life's dangers, deceptions and traps.

Proverbs contains words of wisdom, standards of education, positions of morality and truth expressed in a form of human conduct. This conduct is predicted to provide a general outcome in life, explained by the term, all things being equal. It must be understood that the outcomes of the general but powerful directions for conduct in life will always depend on human behavior and events. Human behavior is so complex and the events of life are so numerous, entangled and complicated that it's not possible to provide a one to one cause and result of human behavior. However, what Solomon does provide is that all things being equal the probabilities of success, happiness, wealth and Godly guidance and protection will be provided to each individual who generally and consistently strives to follow God's plan in the choices of life.

Ultimately all of the wisdom given by Solomon in Proverbs and throughout the Bible finds its final summary and completeness in the life, death and resurrection of Jesus Christ.

> *In him lie hidden all the treasures of wisdom and knowledge.* Colossians 2: 3

Our challenge is to take the wisdom embedded in Proverbs and use it as a guide, a beacon, a light for the dark, obscure, difficult choices of our lives.

STEP 1: CHOICES – REALITY AND GOD

✝

Before we proceed we need to talk about a couple of basic tenets of life. They're very important to our future discussions and understanding. The first of these is that we live in a *Real* world. It's composed of major parts, such as a physical world and a spiritual world. It's crucial to realize that this *Real* world exists and it exists external to the knower. It exists with all of its restrictions and boundaries whether we know about it, understand it, or even care about it. We must understand that this reality will always assert itself! Sometimes it will do so immediately and at other times it will take some time. Yet, it will always occur. We must not be fooled our actions will always have their consequences.

As we grow and mature we build all sorts of ideas how this *Real* world is put together and operates. We begin to believe that we have figured out the world correctly. The problem is, many times we don't really understand how this world operates. Sadly many people don't really care to know, refuse to recognize or believe in its various restrictions and laws.

If a person refuses to believe in the reality that the world works in predictable ways, or is even ignorant of this fact, and lives their life in opposition to reality, the predictable results are they will suffer. The consequences from this can range from general suffering to death.

For instance, we don't have to believe in the law of gravity, which is one of the aspects of the *Real* world. We could climb up on a high building or bridge with intent to jump deciding that the law of gravity doesn't apply to us. However, after we jump the law of gravity immediately comes into play regardless of what we think or feel about it. The law of gravity isn't offended that we aren't a believer. In cold and indifferent ways the laws of our *Real* world operate. We can be a believer or a non-believer; it doesn't make any difference to the law itself.

It's important to know all *Real* world laws, like the law of gravity, always operate predictably. We must instruct our children about life and all of the realities in our *Real* world. In this *Real* world there are spiritual, physical, nutritional, intellectual, and emotional realities, each with its own special laws and boundaries.

There are spiritual realities that are just as real and important as gravity. One of these is that God exists, that he is Spirit, and that he has spiritual laws for us to follow.

> *For God is Spirit, so those who worship him must worship in spirit and in truth.* John 4:24

> *You must diligently obey the commands of the Lord your God—all the laws and decrees he has given you.* Deuteronomy 6: 17

If we miss any of these, either out of ignorance or defiance, then we will suffer for it just as if we stepped off of a high place, ignorant of the law of gravity. To defy any of the physical or spiritual laws of the *Real* world has consequences. If we teach children about these realities and how to operate within their boundaries, then they will have a better chance for a successful and safe life. If we don't teach them about these natural and spiritual laws, they will be the ones to suffer.

Such is the backdrop for the concept of this book, *Choices*. We must be taught to understand the natural and spiritual choices that determine our success or failure in this *Real* world.

> *For we are not fighting against flesh-and-blood enemies, but against evil rulers and authorities of the unseen world, against mighty powers in this dark world, and against evil spirits in the heavenly places.* Ephesians 6: 12

Proverbs is a powerful book that provides instruction and guidance in how an individual should be educated and disciplined to function in the *Real* world. It gives important tips and hints about what's important in life and how to design a plan for successful living. We will call this Proverb's Plan. I will take the reader step by step through Proverb's Plan on how to build a successful life. This plan begins with the most important step in the whole sequence. That step is to understand and accept the fact that there is a God.

God is personal and wants to be involved in our lives and help each of us have the best life possible. We need to acknowledge God for who he is, listen to him, and give him proper respect and authority. When this is done God blesses us and stands with us throughout life's journey.

Fear of the Lord is the beginning of knowledge. Proverbs Ch1 v7

Trust in the Lord, do not depend on your own understanding, and He will direct your path. Ch3 v5

The Lord sees clearly what a man does, examining every path he takes. Ch5 v21

Those who search for me will surely find me. Ch8 v11

The Lord protects the upright but destroys the wicked. Ch10 v29

God rescues the godly from danger, but he lets the wicked fall into trouble. Ch11 v8

Godly people find life; evil people find death. Ch11 v19

The Godly can look forward to happiness, while the wicked can expect only wrath. Ch11 v23

Godliness helps people through life, while the evil are destroyed by their wickedness. Ch13 v6

Those who fear the Lord are secure... Ch14 v26

The Lord is watching everywhere, keeping His eye on both the evil and the good. Ch15 v3

The Lord is far from the wicked, but he hears the prayers of the righteous. Ch15 v29

Fear of the Lord gives life, security and protection from harm. Ch19 v23

The Godly walk with integrity… Ch20 v7

There are other verses in Proverbs that reinforce the issue, but it's clear that to acknowledge God and to follow him provides a distinct and clear plan that gives one an advantage in living in the *Real* world.

Another aspect of the *Real* world involves our emotions. They are of profound importance as we navigate the course of our lives and are a powerful part of human reality. They impact us in a myriad of diverse ways. They involve feelings of anger, fear, hate, love, jealousy, envy, passion, intuition, revenge, fury, sympathy, empathy, joy, upset, temptation, greed and the list goes on and on. Emotions add a great deal to the human condition. Some of these emotions are positive and enhance our lives and others are negative and can impact our lives in very serious ways.

Just as the law of gravity has certain unchangeable and absolute aspects, so do the laws that govern our emotions. The first aspect of emotions is they can hit us quickly with intense feelings and then can rapidly motivate thoughtless behavior. If care isn't taken these quick and intense emotions can overpower our behavioral thought processes and cause us to act with results that may be harmful.

For example, when driving on a busy Interstate highway and a car cuts between you and other cars, the result is you slam on your brakes to keep from hitting the cars involved. Your emotions quickly bring on feelings of anger and fear. This can result in road rage where physical fights and even shootings commonly take place.

Another example might be when an individual is in a long-term relationship, with strong emotional feelings of love and trust, only to discover their partner is cheating. Once again emotional feelings might move the individual to actions that can be violent and destructive that overpower logic and reason.

Of course we can have emotions that can generate joy and love in our experiences. They can motivate a special positive force called humor that can also enhance our lives and make them fuller and more satisfying. So our emotions hold great promise for good but also possible harm for our lives.

The second important law of our emotions is that they have no quality of intelligence to them. They are neither smart nor dumb, they are just very strong intense feelings. Thus, emotions can't be trusted to give us proper guidance for our choices in life. This is a powerful lesson to learn. Emotions can't be trusted! When we experience them it's always wise to stop any action and for a period of time – do nothing! They have been described by certain idioms. These include common ones such as "count to ten" when you are angry, "sleep on it" before you purchase that new car or "don't count your chickens before they hatch."

The point is that emotions can't be trusted! It's common for humans to run a range of emotions throughout the day. One might feel that their boss is mad at them; or something bad might happen to a loved one; an ill parent won't get better; there won't be enough money for retirement; the weight will never come off! These are all feelings or emotions that build within us. The truth is that there are hundreds more that pass through our minds on any particular day.

Remember, emotions can be intense and powerful but they can't be trusted. We'll never be successful in life if we let our emotions govern or control our lives. We must learn to control, manage and channel our emotions with our cognitive abilities. We must think about emotions and separate what facts might be in them from all the lies and falsehoods that help make up the mass of raw emotional power present.

We're beings that are in a constant struggle between our emotional feelings and our intellectual processes. The wise person has learned to develop a balance in life between their emotions and their rational choices. Emotions can be fun, exhilarating, pleasing and joyful. Yet, they can bring on feelings of envy, hatred, jealousy, and revenge. Remember, emotions have no intelligence or thought connected to them. We must separate the worthwhile emotions from those that would be harmful to us or to others. We must pause, resist the strong flood of feelings for quick action, and take the needed time to apply thoughtful and smart choices into the emotional mix.

There are those in society who for various reasons have given up on thoughtful problem solving and the use of intelligent choices to govern their lives. They have allowed emotions to run unrestricted. Their life is controlled almost entirely by emotions.

They could be given ninety-nine rational choices and one emotional choice and they would pick the emotional choice every time. These individuals will never be happy because negative feelings overpower them. They consider themselves victims and have given up on thinking through how to make their lives better. Unless their logical processes are reengaged and they begin to take control of their lives again, the individual will sink deeper into pain and failure. This condition can be reversed but usually not without the help of a professional who can slowly introduce rational choices and hope back into their lives.

Proverbs tells us to make plans and to look ahead in our life and build a future based on Godly principles not emotions. This is a thoughtful, logical process that leaves little room for emotions that could derail us. Strong emotions can come upon us without warning. They can be the force that moves us into actions that can be devastating. An emotional impulse that moves us to thoughtless action can bring trouble into our life. With emotions it will do no good to ask the question, "Why did you do that?" or "What were you thinking?" Because the answer is the person wasn't thinking, he/she was emoting. Their actions were driven by thoughtless emotions that didn't involve the thinking process in any way.

At other times we may, have feelings of hopelessness, failure, worthlessness, that we have disappointed God, lost our salvation, failed our family, etc. Remember that these are emotions and usually have no origin in thought. We need to fight these emotions and deal with them with our brains, our problem solving abilities. If we examine these feelings with thoughtful logic and reason we'll discover that most of what we having been feeling is misleading or wrong. There may be just enough facts in each emotional topic to spin us up, but in total these emotions are false and unnecessarily damning.

Remember, emotions can't be trusted. They can be enjoyed or even raise a red flag concerning our life, but they can't be relied upon to guide us in life's pathways. We must fight transient emotions and replace them with the thoughtful facts of our life. If we live our life guided mostly by emotions rather than careful cognitive direction we'll live a life of pain and failure.

Wise people think before they act; fools don't and even brag about it! Ch13 v16

...the prudent carefully consider their steps. Ch14 v15b

The wise are cautious and avoid danger; fools plunge ahead with great confidence. Ch14 v16

Step 2: Choices – Consequences

The second step in developing a plan for life based on Proverbs is to understand and operate our lives with the realization that it's the choices that we make that determine what our life will become. Choices are the steps of life that take us to our ultimate destination. In our lives, there is neither luck nor chance, only the consequences of our choices. Proverbs warns us to be thoughtful about our choices in life and to use wisdom and understanding based on Godly principles to guide us. The cumulative choices of our lives will make us who we are.

The next step is to choose a partnership with God. However, before talking about that partnership let me make a couple of points concerning conflicts and boundaries. Too many times the different aspects of the *Real* world will present conflicts within our lives. If we were one or two-dimensional creatures that would make it much easier, but such isn't the case. We are multi-dimensional creatures with many of these different dimensions in opposition. Therefore we are always in constant struggle within ourselves concerning what choices we should make. We are creatures of conflict and struggle.

We struggle over choices concerning our job, spouse, children, finances, education, retirement, health, exercise and the list goes on. The biggest conflict of all is the one between good and evil; between what God wants us to do and what Satan wants us to do. These are choices between our spiritual dimension and the evil influence that is always present.

> *The old sinful nature loves to do evil, which is just opposite from what the Holy Spirit wants. And the Spirit gives us desires that are opposite from what the sinful nature desires. These two forces are constantly fighting each other, and your choices are never free from this conflict.* Galatians 5: 17

So, here we find ourselves, creatures of choice; but choice that is in constant conflict and struggle for our future. Our successes or our failures all hang on the thin cord of our choices. It's a daunting undertaking but it's nevertheless our reality. It only ups the ante for thoughtful choices in our lives.

We have all heard the old saying "It isn't over until it's over!" That is so very true in the human condition. We are placed in the dilemma of constantly having to choose the direction of our life with the tension and conflict of our choices. Thus knowing that the consequences of these choices will be with us forever. We can't call a timeout or push the pause button, our choices and their conflicts continue moment by moment until the day we die.

> *Now listen! Today I am giving you a choice between prosperity and disaster, between life and death.* Deuteronomy 30:15

> *...Choose today whom you will serve...But as for me and my family, we will serve the Lord.* Joshua 24:15b

STEP 3: CHOICES – BOUNDARIES

Every aspect of our life is surrounded by boundaries or limitations. A wise person understands this fact and tries to take these boundaries into consideration when making life choices. However, there is a conflicting characteristic regarding boundaries. This problem is that as boundaries are approached there is an increase in excitement.

It's like walking up close to the edge of the Grand Canyon. There is a flow of adrenaline and a rush that comes as one looks at this marvelous sight and the danger that comes with being so near the edge. My family has seen this sight at the Grand Canyon many times, always standing behind the safety of the guardrail. I never was really tempted to leave the safety of the guardrail, climb over it and move closer to the canyon's edge.

However, this isn't the case for some people. Over the years there have been many deaths at the Canyon as people left the safety of the guardrail and moved too close to the edge. There is a life truth that can be learned here. Guardrails have a purpose for being in existence. It doesn't matter if they are located on a bridge, a road, Grand Canyon or a warning given by God. The truth is that individuals cross them at their own peril.

There is a saying among the pilot community, "There are bold pilots and there are old pilots, but there are no old bold pilots." I've been a pilot for almost fifty years and I tried over the years to fly well within the boundaries of my limitations knowing that the unusual or unexpected may very well come during a flight. It might be that the cloud ceiling may become too low, the winds become too high, fuel becomes short, or an emergency might arise with the aircraft's systems. By choosing to fly well within my boundaries, should an emergency develop, I am in a better position to deal with it.

I've had unexpected and multiple problems while flying. Fortunately, their outcomes were successful. These events in my flying are rare because I prepare for problems and try to stay within the safe side of the guardrail.

Every person has limitations in the multiple facets of their life. They involve every dimension of our being. A wise person learns their limitations and the restrictions placed on a Godly life. They plan and execute the plan of their life to stay within the guardrails.

STEP 4: CHOICES – A PARTNERSHIP WITH GOD

We all have the unique ability to think, learn, plan and make informed choices in life that will determine our outcome. We hold tremendous power in our hands to determine our destiny. We can choose to go it alone or invite the God of the universe along to provide much needed help, direction and support.

However, God won't force himself on any of us. We all must decide for ourselves if and when God will be our divine partner in life. The choice always rides with the individual. God wants to be a partner, but only if invited to do so.

A remarkable characteristic of mankind is that we are made in the image of God. Genesis 1: 27 We have several divine attributes that separate us from all of God's other handiwork. Yet, not the least of these is the marvelous ability to think and problem solve. We can think about our past, about our future, about our victories as well as our failures. We can even think on our own thoughts. We can analyze our thoughts and place value on them and even predict with a limited degree of certainty the possible outcomes of the actions or choices that follow. God gave us the capability to think about our lives, our surroundings and the choices that present themselves.

It's this ability to think and to make choices that determines what our life will become. We are responsible for building our future and we do so by the quality of the choices that we make.

> *For we are each responsible for our own conduct.*
> Galatians 6: 5

God talks of the process of wise decision-making and the successful construction of our lives. Matthew 7: 24, Luke 6: 48 He tells us that a wise man builds his house on bedrock and not on sandy ground. The bedrock that God is talking about is his word, principles and teachings. If we're wise we'll make the choices in our lives in concert with these. Our house will be built on that firm foundation that God has laid out for us.

If we make wise Godly choices and build a strong life on God's solid rock we can be assured that when the storms of life come we'll be able to hold firm, be stable and survive.

If on the other hand, we build our homes on the shifting sands of relativism and godlessness, then our homes won't survive the storms and turmoil of life. Our house will collapse as our unstable foundation shifts and gives way to the traumas of life. Our job then is to make wise choices, based on Godly principles, as we build the house of our life.

> *People ruin their lives by their own foolishness and*
> *then are angry at the Lord.* Ch19 v3

> *Do not be deceived, God is not mocked; for whatever*
> *a man sows, that he will also reap.* Galatians 6: 7

An early example of human thinking, problem solving, and house building is found in the book of Genesis. It involves God's second human creation and her name was Eve. She was on her now famous shopping trip to the fruit and vegetable store when she had an encounter and discussion with Satan.

As she was in the produce aisle, Satan began making recommendations for the fruit of the day. He told her that apples were especially good that day and that she should try one. Eve responded that God had told her and Adam that they were free to eat of anything that was in the store, except the apple (Not really apples but the Fruit of the Tree of the Knowledge of Good and Evil.)

God had told her and Adam that if they should ever eat of that tree, there would be very negative consequences. Satan told her no, that God wasn't telling them the truth and on the day that they ate the apple they would be as gods themselves. So Eve chose to bite, as the case would have it, and then offered the newly tasted fruit to Adam. Being a good husband and always eating what was placed before him, Adam also chose to eat the apple.

Now there's a lot to learn about this event and about the consequences that followed, not only for Adam and Eve, but also for the rest of mankind throughout the ages. The first thing that happened was that now Adam and Eve brought all of mankind into a world of the knowledge of good and evil. This brought with it powerful choices with their consequences.

We will forever be creatures who will have to choose between good and evil. This means that we have to build our lives and futures each and every day. We become the product of our decision-making – our choices.

If we partner with God and choose positive moral solutions and make constructive choices that help build our lives in positive ways, then our lives will grow stronger, fuller and more successful. However, if we make bad choices, or drift aimlessly in a sea of moral relativism, we enter a future that promises danger, failure and possible destruction.

A very important part of reality is presented here. It's that we will, all things being equal, always become the product of our choices. I call them our conscious choices that will make or break us! Each and every decision we make moves us along one of two important roads, the road to success and accomplishment or the road to failure and loss.

Many of the decisions that we make each and every day aren't rocket science, but they do accumulate and in summation build our character and define who we are and what we will become. Good choices will always be constructive and healthy and bad choices will always be harmful and eventually painful.

We are warned in Proverbs, *Can a man scoop fire into his lap and not be burned?* Ch6 v27 Seriously, this isn't talking about a dumb party trick but about the consequences that can be expected when we make bad moral or ethical choices.

It's important to stress again, we are free moral agents and responsible for the development of our lives. This is done by the choices we make. Eve's first trip to the fruit-stand started out innocent and ordinary, but turned into a life-changing event for her, Adam and all mankind. Eve's choice to partner with Satan just once, instead of God, changed the world forever.

Just one bad choice in our life can have profound effects on our future. Humans are always in danger in the choices that they make. We need to remember that a life built on good choices can be destroyed if we make one or two bad choices. Over the years I have had friends that made thousands of great choices but in a moment of weakness made two or three bad ones and their lives were shipwrecked. So remember, it isn't over until it's over. We must always be on guard or in a state of readiness. Just like a person in combat who's constantly aware of his/her surroundings. Their head is always turning to see if the enemy is around ready to destroy. We must remain in this same vigil to continue to make wise choices.

Another truth that came from this encounter between Eve and Satan is that now there is evil in the world. Satan introduced evil to mankind. Let me repeat that for those who haven't accepted a *Real* world reality; there is a powerful force, often named evil, that exists in the world and only cares about tearing down and hurting those whose lives it touches.

There's no way around it. One can deny it or try to just explain this evil away as bad luck, bad karma, or the government. (I won't argue this one.) The fact remains that there is a powerful force that is constantly working to destroy each and every human, family, and beneficial institution.

You can call it what you like, Satan has many names, but don't ever forget that evil is present and stands ready to destroy you and everything you hold dear. Evil is an active force seeking 24/7 to corrupt your choices in life and ultimately your future.

> *Be sober, be vigilant; because your adversary the devil walks about like a roaring lion, seeking whom he may devour.* I Peter 5: 8

One other consequence came from this brief but important interaction. Because of the bad choices made by Adam and Eve we have to work hard our entire lives. God made it clear to man he would now have to live by the sweat of his brow to make a living. "Ouch," so much for living off the government.

I know what working by the sweat of your brow feels like. I grew up in Oklahoma and began working outside in the summer sun at age 15. The Oklahoma summer heat and humidity will make a believer out of anyone. Most working people know what life is like. So the lesson to take away from this is that life is hard and we must earn our keep by the sweat of our brow.

No real surprise here, God told Adam and Eve that because of their bad choice in disobeying him they would have to work for a living the rest of their lives and that working would be hard. The sooner an individual learns this reality and accepts it, the better life is going to be.

Our lives, all things being equal, become the grand total of our choices. I say all things being equal, because there may be catastrophic events that invade our lives that are not of our choosing. They can rock and temporarily traumatize our personal worlds. They may require difficult and hard, unforeseen choices to overcome.

However, the choices are ours on how we react and overcome these unforeseen events. It's not what happens to us, but how we react, that will determine our future. We decide, hopefully with God's help, what and who we will become. We must learn to take responsibility. We aren't honest with ourselves if we try to blame others for poor progress in our lives. We need to own up and take responsibility for our lives. It's the only way we can make progress and begin to grow stronger and healthier.

You see, like Eve, you never know what your day is going to bring. For her, it all started as just another shopping trip and it ended with the fall of mankind. We all need to be careful every day to keep partnering with God and making good choices.

Step 5: Choices – Truth

Proverbs reminds us that God's truths are reality and are available to us as we partner with him in making the choices of our lives. We live in a time when society tells us that truth is relative, unstable and dependent on any given situation; that God isn't important and those who trust in him are only stuck in the myths and superstitions of the past.

That isn't what is taught in Proverbs. Solomon expresses the belief that God's truth is absolute. Everything God says and does can be counted on as true, unchanging and immutable.

Every word of God proves true... Ch30 v5

Our children are taught in modern school classrooms that truth and moral standards are relative and depend on a given situation and on the times in which one lives. These are lies that are as old as time. God told Eve that if she and Adam ate from the Tree of the Knowledge of Good and Evil that they would surely die. Genesis 3: 3 Satan told Eve that it wasn't true. He said that God was lying and that there was another truth. Adam and Eve trusted Satan more than God that day and ate from the tree and mankind and the world fell into sin.

God's Truth is not relative but absolute. It can be written with a capital T. God's Truth isn't dependent on either time or condition. Solomon states: *Truth stands the test of time...* Ch12 v19 God's Truth can be counted on as absolute and final. It doesn't change with time or different situations of mankind.

This seems hard for many to understand and accept, because we want to be the exception, or we want a freedom for ourselves that isn't dependent on God. We have been made by God to be free moral agents but always within the boundaries of God's Truth. But we want to go further and have the power and freedom to build and set our own truths and moral standards.

We want to have that power and ability but curiously we don't want others to have it. We want to be the exception. We're taught and get comfort from modern teachings that this is certainly the situation. However it's just not true. God gives us the right and Truthful answers to life's questions.

> *We can gather our thoughts, but the Lord gives the right answer.* Ch16 v1

His commands and teachings provide us a lamp, a light to guide us on our journey through life.

> *For these commands and this teaching are a lamp to light the way ahead of you.* Ch6 v23

However, the choice to choose his way, or not, is always an option. If we use his light it will provide us a true and correct guide that will help keep us out of the traps and hazards of life.

If we refuse his light and guidance then we'll fall victim to many sins, traps and dangers that present themselves throughout our lives. Proverbs calls this living the life of a fool. We hate the word fool in our modern language and in our daily discussions. No one likes to be called a fool. We certainly wouldn't like it used as a description of our life or of our conduct. However, God won't be mocked and he doesn't lie. He lays out the Truth for us in clear and uncertain terms. The way we live our life is certainly our choice, which is why it's so important that all of us, but especially our children, know God's Truths. He can be relied upon to tell us the way things really are.

> *Let me give you common sense. O foolish ones, let me give you understanding. Listen to me! For I have excellent things to tell you. Everything I say is right, for I speak the truth and hate every kind of deception.* Ch8 v5-7

> *Keep the commandments and keep your life; despising them leads to death.* Ch19 v16

Get the truth and never sell it; also get wisdom, discipline and discernment. Ch23 v23

Proverbs provides us God's Truth, his absolute and dependable Truth. God is faithful to teach us the right pathways of life, to provide a light to help us travel that path, and faithful to help us along its dangerous and difficult journey. Accepting God's word as true is a basic step in Proverb's plan for us to make good choices in our partnership with him.

Your word is a lamp for my feet and a light for my path. Psalm 119: 105

STEP 6: CHOICES – A MEANINGFUL LIFE

Proverbs Ch1 v2-4 states that its purpose is to teach people wisdom, discipline and understanding as part of its plan for life. Through Proverbs people receive instruction in discipline and how to do what is right, just and fair. These Proverbs give knowledge and purpose to the young.

We all need a purpose in our lives. A purpose that provides meaning and direction is vital. It's a kind of psychological glue that holds our life together when times get tough. Proverbs provides a clear plan to develop and use this spiritual glue. This is so important at any time in history but it seems particularly relevant in our day.

Young people seem to be absorbed in so many trivial things. The purpose and direction for many seems missing or at the very least cloudy and out of focus. Many of the young are willing to miss and waste opportunity after opportunity available to them. Tragically, there are times when these opportunities are gone, and they may never be available again.

STEP 7: CHOICES – WISDOM

A year
gives you
365
opportunities

God is clear as he speaks in Proverbs about what our choices are regarding wisdom. God wants all of us to be wise and to learn to trust him. However, we must want wisdom and make a choice to receive it from God. We must listen, work and learn about wisdom from an all knowing, loving, and wise God. If we choose not to do this, then our choices will bring consequences that will be devastating. God gives us a clear choice!

> *Wisdom shouts in the streets. She cries out in the public square. She calls out to the crowds along the main street, and to those in front of city hall. "You simpletons!" she cries. "How long will you go on being simpleminded? How long will you mockers relish your mocking? How long will*

you fools fight the facts? Come here and listen to me! I'll pour out the spirit of wisdom upon you and make you wise.

"I called you so often, but you didn't come. I reached out to you, but you paid no attention. You ignored my advice and rejected the correction I offered so I will laugh when you are in trouble! I will mock you when disaster overtakes you – when calamity overcomes you like a storm, when you are engulfed by trouble, and when anguish and distress overwhelm you.

"I will not answer when they cry for help. Even though they anxiously search for me, they will not find me. For they hated knowledge and chose not to fear the Lord. They rejected my advice and paid no attention when I corrected them. That is why they must eat the bitter fruit of living their own way. They must experience the full terror of the path they have chosen. For they are simpletons who turn away from me – to death. They are fools, and their own complacency will destroy them. But all who listen to me will live in peace and safety, unafraid of harm." Ch1 v20-33

Doing wrong is fun for a fool, while wise conduct is a pleasure to the wise. Ch10 v23

To acquire wisdom is to love oneself; people who cherish understanding will prosper. Ch19 v8

Keep the commandments and keep your life; despising them leads to death. Ch19 v16

A major component of a strong and healthy life is one in which life choices are made from the vantage point of wisdom. We need to be wise in the common everyday decisions as well as the life changing ones. It will take wisdom to tell the difference.

My child, listen to me and treasure my instructions. Tune your ears to wisdom, and concentrate on understanding.

*Cry out for insight and understanding. Search for them as
you would for lost money or hidden treasure.* Ch2 v1-4

Once again, this isn't rocket science, to be successful in life we need to learn the right things to do and then do them, to choose and act with wisdom. God's word is full of very important suggestions, principles, commandments and even tips that tell us the best way to direct our lives. To learn its godly advice and to bring it into the everyday choices we make is to act with wisdom. This is powerful stuff! Jesus said, *And you will know the truth, and the truth will set you free.* John 8: 32

God tells us in Proverbs the importance of wisdom and how valuable it is in our lives. We are warned to teach it to our children and then to make every decision with it as our guidepost, or to use modern examples, our Global Positioning System (GPS). While using God's word for guidance, just like a GPS in navigating a car or plane, it's really hard to get lost. I guess one could get lost with a GPS, but would really have to work hard to do so.

The point is that navigation is so easy now that we can see where we are on a GPS moving map. Well, with God's word and with his instruction in Godly wisdom we can do the same thing. We can see where we are, where we need to go and how to get there. Yes, we can get lost in life, if we lose contact with God and lose his guidance. We need to learn of God's wisdom, follow it in the decisions of our lives and keep the faith that it's going to take us where we need to go.

I know this sounds easy and I don't mean to imply that it is. Remember what I told you earlier, life is hard! We'll all have storms that tear through our lives. We'll become ill, lose jobs, lose loved ones, and be hit with failure experiences and a host of other issues and challenges. It's going to hurt. God never said that it wouldn't. You're going to have pain and suffering. You're going to get off course.

Remember that there is evil in the world and that evil wants you off course, down and out and running on an empty tank of faith. Don't give up, get back on course, and remember the true and wise things that you have learned from God in his word. Keep the faith and with God's help get back in the game. Don't ever forget who is pulling for you. God himself! He is the one who said, *I will never leave you nor forsake you.* Hebrews 13: 5.

You may make bad or dumb choices but you can always ask forgiveness, recover and get back on course. God wants that as much as you do and always stands ready to forgive, heal and restore. Learn of his ways and of his wisdom and use them to guide your life choices.

The importance of Wisdom as it concerns our lives is a major component in Proverb's plan. Solomon believed it was of tremendous value. However, wisdom isn't a word used much in conversations today. We don't have discussions on how it's developed or achieved and its importance in our lives. For example, when was the last time someone with whom you were having a conversation remarked, "Hey, how is wisdom coming along in your life? Are you exploring it in your reading and discussions? Are you feeling wiser this year?" Or have you told someone lately, "I've really grown in wisdom this week. I've been putting wise thought into all of my actions."

My belief is that you haven't had conversations like these in a long time, if in fact you ever have. It's not because we don't believe that being wise is a good thing. It's just that in the modern world we don't believe being wise or developing wisdom is worthy of much thought. Yet, wisdom is extremely important in our lives. It's vital to being productive in a very complex and complicated world. It's important to our individual and collective survival. How we handle demanding and critical decisions with wisdom can make all the difference in our world.

What is wisdom? It isn't a set of facts that can be memorized or applied like addition or subtraction in mathematics. There isn't a course in college titled Wisdom 101. Wisdom isn't something that we were born with; rather it's a trait or process that must be learned, developed and practiced through experience. The first step is learning about God by interacting with his word and finding its place in our life. God's wisdom must become assimilated into every thought that we have and into every choice or behavior that we exhibit.

> *Reverence for the Lord is the foundation of true wisdom. The rewards of wisdom come to all who obey him.* Psalm 111: 10

Wisdom is a way of interacting intelligently, successfully and morally with reality. As we move through life we're constantly given a series of dilemmas or problems to solve. These actually begin at birth when as a baby we begin to interact in the world and try, with limited resources, to get our needs met. Needs like, how do I get warm and dry or how can I get something to eat around here? As we get older, sometimes the problems or critical daily events present themselves even before we can get that first cup of coffee. This quickly becomes serious; you would think that problems could wait until at least the second cup of coffee before they present themselves. But we digress. It's how we attack these issues and problems and solve or at least resolve them that establishes our display of wisdom. The display of wisdom, or sometimes lack of it, comes from the experiences that we've already encountered and how successful we've been in dealing with them.

In childhood we begin to solve small problems, the failures and successes that we experience will begin to build a primitive supply of wisdom. These become a pattern of operating, a tiny reservoir of problem solving abilities and coping skills that begin to define us.

When we fail at something it's still a possible learning experience and we can grow in wisdom from it. When we succeed at solving a problem we also grow from that experience. So failure and success both have strong potential learning opportunities that can help us grow in wisdom.

Godly wisdom is the ability to interact with life experiences in such a way that proper paths are taken, clear roads to growth are selected, and progress is achieved. Godly wisdom is boldly taking advantage, in a moral way, of the opportunities that present themselves at the various stages of our lives.

Another important concept in building wisdom involves the issue of timing. We've all heard that timing is everything. Well, everything or not, it's very important in the development of wisdom. In a timely fashion life provides us *doors of opportunity.*

These doors of opportunity are very special events in our lives. They provide opportunities that move our lives forward, sometimes at a very significant pace. They begin a foundation that can be built upon for the rest of our years. God wants us to be wise and to make the most of every opportunity.

> *Be very careful, then, how you live—not as unwise but as wise, making the most of every opportunity, because the days are evil.* Ephesians 5: 5 (NIV)

For example, significant doors of opportunity involve children moving from elementary grades to high school and on to higher education. There are so many of these doors of opportunity during ones younger years it's impossible to list all of them. These include learning to read and master math, science, language, music, and athletic skills. It should include training on how to interact and get along with people. Learning to cope with people of all ages, with varied personalities, is a vital skill set for the development of wisdom.

Those who squander these early open doors in their lives will suffer from needed skills and wise decision-making. A person who is acting with wisdom during these years is one who takes advantage of these open doors to become as well-educated and socially mature as possible.

A wise youth works hard all summer; a youth who sleeps away the hour of opportunity brings shame. Ch10 v5

For you see, these doors of opportunity, even though they're many and seem forever presenting themselves, are actually limited and available only for a finite time. They have a limited shelf life and will at some point close. Many of these doors are very, very hard to reopen once they are closed. Some can never be reopened and will limit human intellectual and psychological development.

Human tragedy starts to reveal itself when multiple doors of opportunity are missed and their advantages lost. This leaves a human being with limited potential and with an ever-growing chance of human failure. These closed doors of missed opportunity build on themselves and the results can be devastating. This failure results in the inability of a person to properly take care of him/her self, to earn a living wage or to establish and maintain a secure and stable family. They may include, dropping out of school early, not learning to read or perform math operations, not developing a career, not learning good work habits, and the list goes on and on.

There are also doors that provide harmful opportunities! These are dark and dangerous doors that when opened and entered by a young person can cause great harm. These pathways can cripple development and progress for the rest of ones life. The use and abuse of drugs, alcohol or sex at an early age and maturity level can be devastating to teens. Use of drugs that cause brain damage, a fatal car accident that involved alcohol by a teen or an unwanted teen pregnancy will change a life forever.

These events usually have lasting traumatic results! Doors of damage and harm will openly present themselves during these young and important years. How Godly wisdom is applied during this time will be most vital for safety and proper intellectual, spiritual and moral development. Wisdom will keep one clear of these dangerous doorways that can deny or close off future opportunities.

> *Happy is the person who finds wisdom and gains understanding. For the profit of wisdom is better than silver, and her wages are better than gold. Wisdom is more precious than rubies; nothing you desire can compare with her. She offers you life in her right hand, and riches and honor in her left. She will guide you down delightful paths; all her ways are satisfying. Wisdom is a tree of life to those who embrace her; happy are those who hold her tightly.* Ch3 v13-18

Choosing Doors of Opportunity

Joe came into my science class with little or no fanfare. From the very first day he made it clear by his actions that he wasn't going to do anything in class. He did no academic work and didn't attempt to contribute to the class! Joe just sat in his chair and found little things to consume his attention.

I talked with him and tried everything I could think of to make a connection and motivate him to try and do at least some work. Nothing seemed to help Joe turn on to school. He wouldn't disturb class in any way, nor would he make a contribution to the class.

Week after week went by with no change in Joe's behavior. I talked with him, his parents, his teachers, and fellow students but still no clue was found to help Joe be successful in class. Soon the weeks added up, and the year came to an end. I felt like everything that I had done to help Joe was just wasted effort.

School was out and summer began. I have to admit that I thought very little about Joe. But when I did, I was frustrated that I hadn't been able to make any change in him. One thing did become a reality to me. I just knew that if he could become motivated that he could make something out of himself and be successful.

Sooner than any teacher would like to believe, summer was over and school began. I received my class list and began to look at the names of the students in my classes and to see how many students had enrolled in them. As every teacher knows, these are two very important realities to check before classes begin.

Well, there was Joe enrolled in my class again. I wondered if he would be any different this year. The year started and Joe began his usual behavior. No work! I began to realize how much I cared about Joe and how much potential he had that was being lost. Once again, I talked with him about his lack of effort, but no response at all. He just looked straight ahead, smiled, and talked about something unrelated to the topic.

It was our practice in school to have what we called a Student Study Team (SST) every three or four weeks. During these SST's all teachers and staff members discussed each student's academic progress, personal situation, attendance, discipline record, etc. If, after an extended time of attempting to help any students become successful, we failed to help them, we voted to either keep the student for more time or to kick them out and refer them to another program that might be more successful.

Well, when Joe's name came up for discussion, I was a little shocked. Quickly, the tone began to develop that the staff didn't believe that Joe should stay at our school but should be moved to another program. They wanted to kick him out! I couldn't believe the staff wanted to kick Joe out! Or maybe it was that I couldn't believe how much I wanted to take his side and defend him.

I understood the frustration of the staff but I just couldn't give up on him! So, I fought to keep Joe for another grading period to see if he would change. Why I thought that he would improve in another three to four weeks when he hadn't done anything for over a year was not clear to me, but somehow, I just knew that he needed more time with us. After a long and heated discussion it was decided that Joe could stay for another grading period. I could hardly wait to talk with Joe the next day. I really didn't know what I was going to say. But I did know that if his academic performance didn't improve, he would be gone in a matter of weeks.

Tomorrow quickly came and there was Joe sitting in his regular seat, doing nothing! I could hardly wait to talk with him while I continued to try and find the right words to get through to him about the seriousness of his situation. I waited until the class was over before I asked Joe if I could have a minute of his time. He agreed verbally but never moved a muscle. As soon as the room was clear I went up to him and explained what had happened the day before in the SST.

I quickly but firmly explained to him that he was in real trouble! Yesterday the staff had discussed his situation and almost kicked him out of the school. The staff made it very clear that if he didn't get busy and start working to graduate that he wouldn't be in the school very long. I explained how I had gone to bat for him and that I had put myself on the line to try and buy him a little more time to get to work and start making academic progress.

As I was railing on him about the situation I could see a change in his expression and an awakening in his emotions. It reminded me of the cartoons when a character gets the light bulb coming on over his head. As I was nearing the end of my speech Joe began to talk out loud. He talked as if he was talking to himself. He said, "I guess I had better start getting to work. I need to graduate from this place!" He continued, "They'll kick me out of here if I don't start working to graduate." It was like he had come to this conclusion all by himself without any help or influence from anyone!

The next weeks and months showed a different Joe! He worked hard at all his assignments. He even decided to work on a science fair project in our class. He did an excellent job on it and even took it to the county science fair and won a medal!

Joe graduated from high school that year. His parents were so proud of him and appreciative of the help he had received at the school.

This could be the end of the story, but there's more. A few months later, I was in my classroom and the door opened. In stepped Joe, his mom, dad and brothers. He had joined the military and had just returned from boot camp. He was all dressed out in his uniform and looked like a million dollars! He, along with his family, were so proud of his accomplishment! They just stopped by to say "Thanks" to a few of his teachers who had worked to help turn his life around. That was a special moment for me! I was so pleased for Joe and his family.

So, as much as you want to, never give up on any human being! They will surprise you! When you think all is over and done, they'll come back and make it happen. They just need someone to keep believing in them and holding their feet to the fire.

Human beings are very special! They can have a hundred negative experiences and be almost defeated when one special caring person can give them the strength to keep going and be successful. So never give up on anyone! You might make all the difference in a life!

Wisdom is the application of one's education, experience, knowledge and personal judgment in the making of a sound decision or quality action. It can be called common sense and common sense may be a product of wisdom. Yet, wisdom seems to go much deeper and cover a lot more human territory. Common sense, even though it doesn't seem to be so common these days, almost leaves the impression that it's something that one is born with or is a gift of birth. Wisdom, as expressed in Proverbs is much more. It's a quality that must be developed and that involves learning by the one who would possess it. It's a choice that must be made by the one who would have it. It's something that must be gained by discipline, hard intellectual work, experience, listening to God and to others, and above all, being willing to learn.

> *The person who strays from common sense will end up in the company of the dead.* Ch21 v16

Proverbs states over and over that there are two types of people. One who prizes and works for wisdom in their life and another who rejects wisdom and what it has to offer. This person is referred to over and over again as a fool. The word moron could also be substituted for the word fool in this context. Proverbs takes this issue of being a fool very seriously and so should we.

> *Don't waste your breath on fools, for they will despise the wisest advice.* Ch23 v9

Wisdom in Proverbs cries out to all offering her benefits, but it's clear that many reject her offer and decide to take the path of foolishness. The result is so clear as we look around in every society, especially our own. Many reject the call to work and gain wisdom in their own lives. The result, as explained in Proverbs, is that each individual who does so will suffer the consequences.

> *For they hated knowledge and chose not to fear the Lord. They rejected my advice and paid no attention when I corrected them. That is why they must eat the bitter fruit of living their own way. They must experience the full terror of the path they have chosen.* Ch1 v29-31

The path to becoming wise is a long one, maybe a life long one. It starts with an important truth that is expressed in Proverbs.

Fear of the Lord is the beginning of wisdom. Knowledge of the Holy One results in understanding. Ch9 v10

Without the knowledge of God and an understanding of our position in the universe and our relation to him we have no hope of becoming wise. He is the holy, all-knowing God of the universe. He is the author and maker of everything that is in existence, including each of us. He loves us and wants to have a meaningful relationship. He wants to teach and guide us as we travel our life's journey. He wants to instruct us to be wise and to conduct our affairs with sound action and good judgment.

Proverbs is clear about these things, but it's also clear that gaining wisdom and traveling our road of life is a choice. Our choice! Here we go again with that choice thing and being responsible for our own lives. Each of us can play the fool and reject God's help and his instruction in wisdom and good judgment. Too many human beings, for whatever multiple reasons, reject the offer to become wise and instead select the path of becoming a fool. "It's unfair," they protest.

Others have accepted the position that they are victims. They say, "What can I do? The circumstances of life have put me in my present situation and there's nothing that I can do about it." They believe that it's somebody else's fault that they are in the position they're in and nothing can be done. How sad this belief and practice is for those involved.

Unless their beliefs are changed and their lives turned around by taking responsibility and making good choices, they'll be doomed to a life of sadness and failure. These individuals view the control of their lives as somewhere outside of themselves. They believe they have little or no control over what happens to them. They are only life's victims!

Yet, Proverbs tells us a different story. Its view is that we are the controllers of our lives. We are in charge! The individual, daily decisions that we make ultimately move us toward success or failure. Proverbs tells a positive story and gives us hope for a better today and tomorrow. Wisdom is available to us, God wants to be our partner in our decision making process. He will leave us alone to do our thing if that's the way we want it, but that isn't God's first choice for us. He wants to give us wisdom. Godly wisdom that can and will change our lives is just waiting for each of us who desire it, seek it and inculcate it into our lives.

If you become wise, you will be the one to benefit. If you scorn wisdom, you will be the one to suffer. Ch9 v12

Proverbs tells us that wisdom and good judgment are ours for the taking. Of course we have to work to develop wisdom and good judgment in our lives, but it's worth the work and effort. We're told that wisdom is worth more than silver and gold, nothing can be compared to it because wisdom is priceless.

For wisdom is far more valuable than rubies. Nothing you desire can be compared with it. Ch8 v11-12

Getting wisdom is the most important thing you can do. Ch4 v7

...leave your foolish ways behind, and begin to live; learn to be wise. Ch9 v6

So then, how does one develop wisdom? Proverbs is clear that it comes from several sources. First, as we have already seen, it comes from recognizing God for who and what he is and putting our lives in proper relationship with Him. We become a partner with God in our journey. Other pieces of the wisdom puzzle that are important include:

Get all the advice and instruction you can, and be wise the rest of your life. Ch19 v20 *Whoever walks with the wise will become wise; whoever walks with fools will suffer harm.* Ch13 v20

The advice of the wise is like a life giving fountain; those who accept it avoid the snares of death. Ch11 v14

Wise people treasure knowledge, but the babbling of a fool invites trouble. Ch10 v14

Those who would become wise must gain all the education and training available to them. They must be willing to learn wisdom from those around them, like their parents, grandparents, teachers, and pastors. We need to remember those *doors of opportunity* that we talked about.

One more major point about wisdom, and it's an important one, is that it gives life. We know from modern science that proper health care and nutrition can add years and provide an improved quality of life. Eating wisely, exercising properly, and following preventive medical practices accomplish these health results.

> *Wisdom will multiply your days and add years to your life.* Ch9 v11

> *Wisdom is a tree of life, …* Ch3 v18

Getting wisdom is much like understanding the effects of aerobic exercise that's been documented and promoted from the early 1960's. The results of regular aerobic exercise such as running, jogging, biking or walking have all become widely known. Aerobic exercise increases cardiovascular health and muscle tone, lowers blood pressure, helps control weight, and decreases the chance of contracting many diseases such as diabetes and cancer. It increases one's self-concept and even seems to retard the aging process and mental decline. Exercise accomplishes so many things to improve our general health that it can be thought of as being almost magic. It isn't magic, but it's magical in maintaining our health and fitness as we mature.

The same can be said of gaining wisdom in our daily lives. Wisdom teaches us to give good advice, use fewer words, be refreshing to others, build a strong psychological house, be mighty in our actions, and be concerned for others. Gaining wisdom also seems to be magical because of all it provides. However, once again, it's not magic but a consequence of our choices and of living our lives in such a way as to gain knowledge and wisdom and use them to direct and control our behaviors. This is wisdom in action. It's ours for the taking. *Wisdom shouts in the streets.* Ch1 v20. The question is, will we listen and follow the requirements to become wise?

Now, to sum up Proverb's view of wisdom as a step in its plan for building a successful life, getting it is the most important accomplishment one can achieve. It's priceless and of great value. It's available to everyone. It's restricted to no one. Yet, there is a Godly requirement, the person who achieves it must want to have it and make the needed effort to make it happen.

Wisdom's Subdivisions

Step 8: Choices – Thinking

The godly think before speaking; the wicked spout evil words. Ch15 v28

    This step in Proverb's plan reminds us that we should be thoughtful before we speak. This is a responsibility of all Godly people. Words have the ability to heal or harm and they should never be used with disregard. We are warned that wicked people spout evil words. This can be a clear sign of a person who isn't following God's principles and plans. It should never be a characteristic of those who claim God as Lord of their lives. Thinking is a trait that separates us from the animals and it's one that also separates us from the wicked. We need to think before we invade the life of others with our words. We need to take this duty and responsibility very seriously.

The question is how can we be thoughtful about our speech and action? The answer is to stop when we are confronted with an issue and just say or do nothing. The silence may be deafening and the desire to act may be compelling. Resist the temptations to do anything. Let the emotions settle down and take a mental break. Sometimes only a few seconds will be required to gain control and begin to think clearly. In other situations more time will be required. If this is the case, once again say nothing but just walk away. There are lots of options here. Go get a cup of coffee, a coke, or even go for a short walk. Take this needed time to think through the situation and consider your options. Don't be in a hurry to say or do anything that you will be sorry for later. It's better to come back to a situation after calming down and thinking through the options than it is to say or do the wrong thing. Be thoughtful, be wise and don't let others push your buttons and cause you to act in a way that you know might be harmful to you or to others.

Be particularly careful not to use words that will harm others. Phrases like, you are stupid, you're just wrong, what's wrong with you, why can't you see it, and a multitude of others shouldn't be used. They tend to tear down the self worth of others and that should never be our goal. If you don't know what to say that will be helpful, just say nothing at all.

> *A gentle answer turns away wrath, but harsh words stir up anger.* Ch15 v1

> *Fix your thoughts on what is true and honorable and right. Think about things that are pure and lovely and admirable. Think about things that are excellent and worthy of praise.* Philippians 4:8b

STEP 9: CHOICES – BECOMING AN INTELLIGENT PERSON

✝

Intelligent people are always open to new ideas. In fact they look for them Ch18 v15

Proverbs says people who want to grow intellectually should always be open to learning new ideas. Those who strive to be more intelligent however, aren't only open to learning new things, but are actively looking for them.

Modern medical research has documented that mental abilities normally decline as we age, but can be delayed or arrested if we stay active physically, mentally, socially and spiritually. It doesn't really matter what activities, as long as the person is exercising their brain by learning new things, and being socially active.

Scientific evidence states that sustained physical activity, such as aerobic exercise, can also be of great intellectual value. It's not so much the limitations of your ability, but your willingness to constantly learn and grow that can help arrest intellectual decline.

STEP 10: CHOICES – A GOOD REPUTATION

Choose a good reputation over great riches, for being held in high esteem is better than having silver or gold. Ch22 v1

Get the truth and don't ever sell it; also get wisdom, discipline and discernment. Ch23 v23

Proverbs teaches that even though money is of value there are other things that are of greater worth. One of the themes in Proverbs is that having all the money in the world with the ability to purchase anything doesn't ensure a good, happy and prosperous life. Of course money is vital, especially in providing the essentials like food, clothing, and shelter. Once these things are secured it's clear that we won't be happy if we neglect other needs in our lives. These would include building a good reputation, gaining in wisdom, discipline and discernment, securing loving relationships, helping others, or in other words, developing our soul! The human condition so often tends to pit the quest for riches against the values of our soul. Proverbs reminds us that making a living is important but that it's not the end in which to live.

STEP 11: CHOICES – SELF-CONTROL

A person without self-control is as defenseless as a city with broken-down walls. Ch25 v28

Self-control is a problem that begins early in life and is part of Proverb's plan. Children learn they can get the attention of adults very quickly by pitching a fit, screaming and yelling. One of their favorite times to do this is when going through the checkout line in a supermarket or a department store. Of course store managers understand that the products that they display along that line such as candy, gum, and balloons will attract the attention of the children. Many parents don't know how to properly respond to the child and will do almost anything to keep them from going berserk. So they give the child what they want and two out of three individuals involved in this situation are happy. If the parents are experienced or trained in how to deal with these situations the child will quickly learn that it will do no good to pitch a fit. If they scream and yell there will be unpleasant results or consequences.

It's important for parents to help their children learn to be self-controlled. No one wants to be around a person who is loud, undisciplined and who loses the ability to control their behavior. This is true in a child but it's especially true in an adult. Self-control is a learned behavior and with it people can manage their life in a way that will be productive and rewarding. Remember, it's all about choices, the everyday choices of your life add up to make you who you become. Make the best choices you can make today in order to be a better and more successful you tomorrow.

STEP 12: CHOICES – RICHES

Don't weary yourself trying to get rich. Why waste your time? For riches can disappear as though they had the wings of a bird! Ch23 v4

Let's face it, money is significant! It doesn't rank up there with oxygen, water or even food, but it's definitely high on the list. The first part of your income that provides food, clothing, and shelter for you and your family is vital. As you continue to make more and more money providing for other things like retirement, savings, and vacation, it starts to become less immediately vital. It's still important, but not like the big three.

There comes a point where more money doesn't provide one with an improved quality of life. Whether you drive a Chevrolet, Ford, or a Mercedes will count very little in the overall value of your life. You may think that it will, but it won't. In fact, driving a Ford and saving the difference between the costs of the Mercedes might improve the quality of life in terms of worry and concern over financial needs. So what Proverb's plan is saying is don't worry and fret over getting so wealthy that it begins to control your life and your choices. Be content with enough to build a solid living for your family both today and in the future. In this regard it's more important how you manage your money than in how much you make.

Proverbs reminds us that riches are fleeting and care and good stewardship should be practiced. Working hard and providing a good income for yourself and your family is a good thing. Be that as it may, good things can become bad things when the handling of them becomes irresponsible. Balance is critical make sure that you live a life that keeps priorities in place. Family relationships are vital and amassing wealth at the expense of the family is a mistake and not a wise choice.

A house is built by wisdom and becomes strong through good sense. Through knowledge its rooms are filled with all sorts of precious riches and valuables. Ch24 v3

The way to get rich in our lives, as mentioned in Proverbs, is to use wisdom and good sense to build our homes. Once again it's our duty to build our families through thoughtful, balanced, and wise choices. We need to remember that after our commitment to God our next responsibility is to our family. These two things must be our highest priority. I know this list is long for an adult. We have to take care of work, house, yard, car, pets, brush our teeth twice a day and even floss once a day. I've said it before, life is hard and the pressure on us is huge and sometimes overwhelming. Balancing priorities, utilizing wisdom and good sense, with God and our families foremost, are the keys to success. There are times that may require possible deviations, but these should be well thought out and planned choices. They should be the exception and not the rule.

Step 13: Choices – Worry

Worry weighs a person down; an encouraging word cheers a person up. Ch12 v25

A glad heart makes a happy face; a broken heart crushes the spirit. Ch15 v13

A person's words can be life-giving water; words of true wisdom are as refreshing as a bubbling brook. Ch18 v4

We all worry about things that go on in our lives. Some of us worry more than others but it's a universal condition in which we find ourselves. The fact is clear that worrying drags us down physically and psychologically. It saps our strength and if our worrying becomes intense or extends for a long period of time, then it's going to affect our health. We may also recognize that the opposite is true. When we're happy and pleased with events going on in our lives we gain strength and tend to be healthier and stronger.

Proverb's plan brings up this obvious fact and goes on to describe how important it is to give words of encouragement to those around us who may be struggling with problems or issues. A kind and encouraging word can work miracles in the lives of others. Sometimes we just don't take the time to realize how important words can be. The things we say hold great power to help or injure. Proverbs reminds us to be encouraging and to cheer others up. It could be as simple as a kind word, sending a card, an email or making a phone call to a friend. We need to understand that the power of words is a valuable human tool that should be used wisely and with caution.

PERSONAL STORY 2

Never Underestimate the Influence You Have on Others!

Several years ago I was teaching biology in a high school in California. I had already taught two classes that morning and this third class was just about over. I was looking forward to the end of the class because I was going to have a short break. It's amazing the little things you can look forward to as a teacher. A quick bathroom break, and a cup of coffee or a diet coke can seem like a rich man's treasure.

I completed the lesson and there was about three minutes left in the class. I decided to walk around the room and talk to as many students as possible. Nothing big, just a little time to give a few of my students "the time of day." I didn't realize at the time how important this was for the students and even for the teacher. I do now!

As I moved down the rows of students, I asked each of them how things were going. They would give responses like "fine", "okay", and "good". I really wasn't listening too closely to their responses, and felt good that all was going well with each of them, at least on a surface level.

Then I came to Pam. I asked her the standard question. "How are you today?" I already was moving on to the next student, expecting the standard reply. Well, Pam didn't give the standard reply. She said, "I'm not doing very well! My family, which is a 'mixed' one, doesn't get along. My step-mom doesn't like me. My half-brothers and sister fight with my sister and me. Our home isn't a happy one with a lot of fighting constantly going on. My step-mom and I had a fight this morning before school and I really don't want to go home this afternoon. I don't like my life right now and I am not looking forward to going home today."

I was speechless! I hadn't planned on a response like this. Pam just looked at me and I could see in her face that she was waiting for me to say something. Just then the bell rang, and by instinct I dismissed the class. Pam just sat in her seat looking at me. I really didn't know what to say. Then the words began to flow from my lips. I was barely aware of what I was saying. I told her I was sorry about her situation at home. I knew that things can get tough in families and sometimes life can seem very hard, but that she was a wonderful person and that she would be able to see this thing through. I told her that she had what it took to get through school and make a life for herself. I then told her I hoped things went better for her and that she had a good day. She left the class and we completed the school year together without another conversation of this type.

The next couple of years passed and Pam graduated from high school. The months went by and I lost track of her. Before I realized it, Christmas time was upon us. My wife and I started getting our usual collection of cards. As I began looking through them I saw a card with a return address that I didn't recognize. It was from a Colorado address. I opened it and to my surprise it was a Christmas card from Pam. She had moved to Colorado and was working at a good job.

She told me something that shocked and taught me more about teaching and the power of human relationships than I had learned in years. She told me how much it had meant to her the day that I took the time to talk with her about her personal problems. It had helped her make it through her family situation and graduate from high school. She said it was so thoughtful of me to take the time from my busy schedule to try and help her. *Wow!* I thought! *I did that?* Of course I hadn't done that much, but to her the little time I gave her was life changing!

For many years after this, I received a Christmas card from Pam. She told me about her new baby and sent a picture of her "pride and joy." She would always remind me again of that one conversation that had such an impact on her life.

We must never underestimate the influence we have on each person with whom we come in contact. They may or may not look up to us and respect us! Yet, they know that we are successful, responsible human beings that can help them. They look to us for direction, support and acceptance! Never forget the power we have to heal or to hurt.

You'll never know when you'll have a Pam in your life that will need "the time of day!" It may come in the check out line at a store, or at your place of work, or someone at church. It could be the most important thing you do all day!

STEP 14: CHOICES – DISCRETION

Discretion is a life-giving fountain to those who possess it, but discipline is wasted on fools. Ch16 v22

Discretion, or the ability to speak in a way that won't offend someone or betray confidential information, is a vital characteristic. Proverb's plan describes it as a *life-giving fountain*, an indispensable characteristic to those who possess it. Sometimes it's hard to tell the truth about events or situations where human feelings and emotions are involved. Words are so powerful and carry with them so much potential for good or for harm. So, to have the ability to deliver an important message without unduly injuring another person is really the gift of wisdom. It's a rare gift that should be highly valued.

STEP 15: CHOICES – DESPISING ADVICE

✝

People who despise advice will find themselves in trouble; those who respect it will succeed. Ch13 v13

I don't know why, but it's hard for most of us to take advice whether it's from Proverbs or from others. I don't know if we are inherently too proud or maybe we think that we already know it all. Since we can't live long enough to make all the mistakes that are possible, it would be wise of us to learn from the experiences of others.

Let me give you an example from the world of flying. My wife and I have flown our airplane all over the United States. We've found ourselves in many wonderful and interesting places. Yet, for varied reasons, some of them are hard to fly into or out of. Reading the charts, approach plates, and information on each of the airports is vital of course; however, there's nothing like calling the airport ahead of time and talking to local pilots. They know the ins and outs of every aspect concerning the airport. Their information can be invaluable for flight safety and efficiency. I try to talk with them whenever it's possible.

The same is true for those who have been down a road of life that we are about to travel. It would be smart of us to go to those more experienced travelers and ask for their advice. Of course we don't have to take it. Maybe it isn't the proper course to take because situations change. In spite of that, it's always worth listening to and considering. At the very least we'll have heard an experienced voice that may provide us some needed insight and guidance.

STEP 16: CHOICES – SIN AND SELF-CONTROL

For the Lord sees clearly what a man does, examining every path he takes. An evil man is held captive by his own sins; they are ropes that catch and hold him. He will die for lack of self-control; he will be lost because of his incredible folly. Ch5 v21-23

Proverb's plan tells us about sin and that it's a reality. No matter how hard we try we all fall short of what God wants us to do. The Bible says it's in our nature to sin. Modern scientists might say *it's in our genes*. We have a built in bias or spin to make bad choices. What's really bad about this is that God sees all of our behaviors and therefore each and every sin we commit. Yikes! We can hide some of our bad behavior from friends and loved ones, but we can't hide a single one from God. If he were a God that just wanted to thump us for bad behavior, then he would be thumping us all day long. Yet, that isn't the case. God is the God of love. Sure, he sees our bad behavior and it hurts him to see it, just like it hurts a parent to see their child doing something wrong. However, he stands ready to forgive and restore us to a fellowship with him.

There is some bad news here. We're creatures of choice and our bad choices can become habits of behavior. If we inculcate these in our lives they can become a vital and constant part of who we are, a bad habit. We can become morally blind to what we're doing. Proverbs describes this as ropes that tie us to our sin and bad behavior. Our bad choices are placed on a kind of autopilot than runs within our lives with little or no conscience awareness of our actions. Proverbs tells us that these foolish acts can ultimately cost us our very lives.

Many men and women repeat destructive choices over and over again and then wonder why their marriage breaks up or why their children are in trouble. Proverbs reminds us that we are biased to move toward sin but that isn't the complete story. We have the power of choice and we can stop the sin and evil behavior and choose to do what God wants us to do. The right thing! The choice of behaviors that brings us closer to God and to our family and friends is possible. We can develop good habits! We don't have to be tied to sin with ropes of uncertainty and despair. Through a choice of dependence on God and the development of behaviors that are right and responsible, we can align our choices and our lives to live in accordance with Proverb's plan.

STEP 17: CHOICES – INTEGRITY AND HONESTY

People with integrity have firm footing, but those who follow crooked paths will slip and fall. Ch10 v9

The Lord hates people with twisted hearts, but he delights in those who have integrity. Ch11 v20

The honest will be rescued from harm, but those who are crooked will be destroyed. Ch28 v18

The next step in Proverb's plan to be successful is to make life choices with honesty and integrity. For starters, human relations, whether personal or professional, can't exist over an extended period of time if they aren't built on honesty and integrity. It takes weeks, months and even years for individuals to build trusting associations. These will be built on hundreds, if not thousands, of choices, interactions and observations. They can be strong and hold promise of a great and successful future; however, if one member displays a behavior, or makes a choice, that's dishonest or lacks integrity, the relationship will be suddenly and severely damaged or destroyed.

A reputation of honesty and integrity takes a lifetime to build and maintain, but unfortunately it takes only a moment of bad choices to destroy. As we make choices that will determine who and what we become, we need to use extreme care to guard that trust. There's nothing in our lives that's more important than honesty and integrity. It's one of those core values that will make us successful in all of life's relationships.

STEP 18: CHOICES – HEALTH

Don't be impressed with your own wisdom. Instead, fear the Lord and turn your back on evil. Then you will gain renewed health and vitality. Ch3 v7-8

Riches won't help on the Day of Judgment, but right living is a safeguard against death. Ch11 v4

A relaxed attitude lengthens life; jealousy rots it away. Ch14 v30

A cheerful look brings joy to the heart; good news makes for good health. Ch15 v30

Kind words are like honey—sweet to the soul and healthy for the body. Ch16 v24

A dry crust eaten in peace is better than a great feast with strife. Ch17 v1

A cheerful heart is good medicine, but a broken spirit saps a person's strength. Ch17 v22

A person's words can be life-giving water; words of true wisdom are as refreshing as a bubbling brook. Ch18 v4

The human spirit can endure a sick body, but who can bear it if the spirit is crushed? Ch18 v14

Words satisfy the soul as food satisfies the stomach; the right words on a person's lips bring satisfaction. Ch18 v20

We've learned a lot about healthy living since Proverbs was written. This includes learning about exercise; utilizing good nutrition; dealing with stress and its consequences; the effects of smoking and alcohol; and many other health related issues. One of those is preventing health problems before they arise. In a recently released health study that was conducted over a 35-year period this position was supported. Those who followed these five simple lifestyle rules: scheduling regular exercise; practicing sensible eating; maintaining a healthy weight; consuming minimal amounts of alcohol; and not smoking saw a huge decrease in health issues and an increase in longevity. The study showed a 70 percent reduction in dangerous health conditions including cancer, heart attacks, strokes, diabetes and dementia. (Elwood, et al., 2013) That is what Proverb's plan is talking about.

There are choices in our lives that will impact our long-term general health. It's a little sad that it's taken so many years and so much scientific research to bring these behaviors to our attention. Of course, there's no guarantee that if we jog everyday, eat lots of fruits and vegetables, and reduce our stress, that we'll live to be 120 years old. However, statistically speaking, and all things being equal, science has demonstrated that if we do these things consistently our health will be positively affected.

We know from research that the opposite is also true, if a person makes multiple poor health choices they can have serious health consequences. These might include putting on an extra hundred pounds; smoking and drinking excessively; not exercising; maintaining poor nutrition; and being constantly stressed out at the job. The health results could range from diabetes, coronary issues, various cancers, breathing problems, joint problems or obesity. Over time this could very well result in premature disability or death. What Proverbs is saying is be wise. First recognize your responsibilities to God, fear him in a respectful way and work hard to live a healthy lifestyle.

> *Don't you realize that your body is the temple of the Holy Spirit, who lives in you and was given to you by God? You do not belong to yourself, for God bought you with a high price. So you must honor God with your body.* 1 Corinthians 6: 19-20

After developing a healthy lifestyle, we should work to live a life of goodness and concern for others. This can be hard to do, but once again it's a choice. We won't be successful at it one hundred percent of the time, but we should work at it all of the time. Forgive yourself when you mess up, seek forgiveness and move on to try and do better. Try to be kind and respectful in your relationship with others. It's one of those things that usually gives back to you. The more you work to be kind and helpful to others the more they will tend to reciprocate.

That doesn't mean that there aren't going to be problems or that everyone will treat you well. Still, many will and it will make the day better. Try to be cheerful and laugh as much as you can with others. Humor is a wonderful thing and it can take the sting out of life's disappointments and hurts.

There has been a lot of scientific research on humor and laughing as it relates to our health. Years ago, Readers Digest coined the term *Laughter is the best medicine* into a popular expression. Proverbs was there first, being happy and cheerful is good medicine. It tells of the importance of words. They can be healing, healthy and sweet to the soul. Of course they can also be the opposite. That's why we must be very careful with the words we use. They can be as damaging as a knife or club. Even more so, for when a hurt is inflicted with a knife it will start to heal immediately. Not so with words, their affects may never heal. The damage they have done can be relived over and over again.

Words are truly tools of healing or hurt. One of the major choices in life should be to use words with care.

A person's words can be life-giving water; words of true wisdom are as refreshing as a bubbling brook. Ch18 v4

Step 19: Choices – Avoiding Life's Traps

The advice of the wise is like a life giving fountain; those who accept it avoid the snares of death. Ch13 v14

Fear of the Lord is a life-giving fountain; it offers escape from the snares of death. Ch14 v27

What I'm going to say I've said before, it's important to constantly keep in mind. There is evil in the world. It's an active force that loves to see human beings get themselves in trouble, traumatize their lives and lead them into the traps and snares of life. You may call it what you like: the devil, sin, human fallibility, original sin, evil, or just human stupidity. The Bible talks a lot about all of these. So, the basic idea is that humans, as they attempt to live their lives in an orderly and productive manner, will run into problems with their behavior and decision-making. A basic truth is that there are dangerous traps in life. I believe that some of these traps are worthy of identification and discussion.

<u>Some of Life's Traps and Lies</u>

Trap # 1: **Life is easy.** Ecclesiastes 7: 14, John 16: 33

Trap # 2: **Parents don't need to discipline their children**. Proverbs Ch13 v24, Hebrews 12: 7

Trap # 3: **The use of alcohol poses no threat.** Ch21 v1, Ch31 v4-6, Genesis 9: 20-29, 19: 30-36, Leviticus 10: 8-11

Trap # 4: **Parents don't need to educate their children spiritually.** Ch4 v10-11, 1 John 2: 1-29

Trap # 5: **Being lazy in life is not a problem.** Ch19 v15, Ch10 v4, Ch10 v26, Ch12 v24, Ch13 v4

Trap # 6: **Children don't need to listen to their parents.** Ch1 v8

Trap # 7: **We don't need to trust God.** Ch3 v5

Trap # 8: **Living a Godly life doesn't have any advantages.** Ch3 v33, Romans 8: 18

Trap # 9: **Husbands and wives don't need to be faithful to each other.** Ch7 v24-27, Ephesians 5: 22-33

Trap #10: **There is nothing wrong with adultery.** Ch6 v24-29, 32-35

Trap #11: **Education isn't important.** Ch1 v24, Ch3 v14-15, 2 Timothy 3:16

Trap #12: **The way we handle money isn't important.** Ch3 v9, Ch6 v1-5, Exodus 22: 29, Malachi 3: 10, Luke 12: 34

Trap #13: **Planning for the future isn't necessary.** Ch22 v3, Ch3 v21

Trap #14: **Educating children about nutrition and exercise isn't valuable.**
1 Corinthians 6: 19-20, 1 Corinthians 6: 12

Trap #15: **Quality, regular family time together isn't essential.** Ch22 v6

Trap #16: **Communication isn't vital.** Ephesians 4: 29

Trap #17: **It's not important to teach children that the tongue is dangerous**.
James 3: 2b, 3: 6

Well, you get the point. I could list more traps and I'm sure that you could add to the list. The point is that there are traps and land mines along the highway of life. Proverb's plan gives excellent advice on how to avoid them and the possible disasters they can bring.

STEP 20: CHOICES – FEAR AND PROTECTION

Fear is a constant companion throughout life. When we were children we feared certain things because of our lack of understanding. Our fears don't go away as we grow older they continue to stay with us. Our fears include concern for: loved ones, jobs, health, children's future, and money. Yet, we're told throughout the Bible, including many times in Proverbs, that we shouldn't be in fear. We're told that God loves us and wants the very best for our lives. He wants a relationship with us that will provide protection from harm and strength to fight the battles that we'll encounter in life.

Fear of the Lord gives life, security, and protection from harm. Ch19 v23

God rescues the godly from danger, but he lets the wicked fall into trouble. Ch11 v8

Godliness helps people all through life, while the evil are destroyed by their wickedness. Ch13 v6

Those who fear the Lord are secure; he will be a place of refuge for their children. Ch14 v26

The name of the Lord is a strong fortress; the godly run to him and are safe. Ch18 v10

A prudent person foresees the danger ahead and takes precautions; the simpleton goes blindly on and suffers the consequences. Ch22 v3

Every word of God proves true. He defends all who come to him for protection. Ch30 v5

Fear of the Lord is a life-giving fountain; it offers escape from the snares of death. Ch14 v27

The Lord protects the upright but destroys the wicked. Ch10 v29

These are just a few of the promises for protection among the hundreds that are in the Bible. God is our ever-present help in times of trouble. We do need to believe in him, do the right things he's told us to do and then have faith that God himself is faithful and will protect us. This doesn't mean that we will never be threatened, be afraid or be in trouble. What it does mean is that we'll have a divine partner throughout our problems and struggles that will help us deal with them.

Fear isn't a bad thing. It's a healthy response to events and situations in life where we should be afraid and on guard. It's a protective device of our make up that rings a bell that all hands are needed on deck. It's a signal that something bad has happened or is about to happen and emergency action is needed now. Fear can save our lives, protect us, and our future. Only a fool ignores fear. It needs to be faced and dealt with in a proper way. God has promised to help us with that. We need to trust God that in the end it's going to be all right. He will see us through every difficult situation in our lives.

Proverb's plan tells us that we need fear only God and really nothing else. This Godly fear isn't fear as we commonly know it, it's a sense of awe and respect. God wants us to respect him and serve him as the one holy God.

Step 21: Choices – Guidance for Our Lives

There's no better assurance given by God in Proverbs than the promise of guidance in the everyday decisions of our lives. These daily decisions, called choices, ultimately make and mold us into the human beings we become. It's important that each and every choice we make, every course of action we take, be those that will build our lives and make us better people. Knowing that God will guide us fills our lives with hope and promise for a better tomorrow.

It's like being on a California freeway and approaching multiple exits that will take us to different destinations. We're traveling at a high rate of speed and have to make rapid decisions on which road or off ramp to take. I've been there so many times and without a second person to help with the navigation it can be overwhelming. We're traveling so fast and the exit ramps come so quickly it can be difficult to make the right choice. Thank God we don't have to travel life's roads alone. God has been down all of these roads and he knows which ones are best, good, fair and bad. He will provide the direction and help if we'll just ask him and listen to him.

However, being human, sometimes we don't take God's direction or won't listen to him and onto the wrong road we go. God won't throw up his hands and say, "Well, what was that all about? I told you and you didn't listen so you're now on your own." God doesn't operate that way, not if we're trying to make the right choices and want to take the right road. He understands that we're weak and sometimes don't get the right signal or just make a bad choice. He's just like a GPS in the car in that he will say, *take the next exit and go back to the last turn*. He's patient with us and wants only the best road for us. If we continue on the wrong road and by our actions tell God we want to follow map directions of our own choosing, he will honor our decisions and let us go our own way. When we finally run out of gas, come to a dead end or get completely lost and throw up our hands and ask God for forgiveness and for help, he stands ready to provide us direction and help.

The word that the Bible uses for this is redemption! It means that God is always ready to reclaim us to himself through his grace and mercy. He has paid the debt for all of our sins through his son Jesus dying on the cross. He wants us back with him; he loves us with an undying love. All we have to do is to choose to ask for forgiveness and be sincere about it. His directions for our lives will begin anew!

> *Commit your work to the Lord, and then your plans will succeed.* Ch16 v3

> *We can make our plans, but the Lord determines our steps.* Ch16 v9

> *You can make all the plans, but the Lord's purpose will prevail.* Ch19 v21

> *Plans succeed through good counsel; don't go to war without the advice of others.* Ch20 v8

Human plans, no matter how wise or well advised, cannot stand against the Lord. Ch21 v30

Whoever pursues godliness and unfailing love will find life, godliness, and honor. Ch21 v21

Unfortunately, there are always consequences for the roads we have chosen. There could be health, interpersonal, financial or spiritual consequences that can damage our lives. God won't give up on us if we're sorry and ask for forgiveness, but he won't shield us from the consequences of our bad decisions.

For they hated knowledge and chose not to fear the Lord. They rejected my advice and paid no attention when I corrected them. That is why they must eat the bitter fruit of living their own way. They must experience the full terror of the path they have chosen. Ch1 v29-31

Step 22: Choices – Godliness

Proverb's plan gives us a clear picture of what to expect when people and nations follow God. If we pursue godliness and honor God, then our nation will be exalted. If we, as a people, fall into sin and turn our backs on God, then we're going to be on our own and God is going to distance himself from us. It seems to be a pattern that when things are going well we tend to drift from God and begin to believe that we can make it on our own. When events go poorly then we begin to wonder where God is and why has he abandoned us. We complain about God and wonder why he isn't helping us.

> *People ruin their lives by their own foolishness and then are angry at the Lord.* Ch19 v3

It's not a rocket science sort of thing. It's clear and simple. If we as Christians follow God's principles and direction, all things being equal, then he will bless us. If we choose not to follow him then there are going to be consequences. This is true both at the individual and at the collective level as a nation. Too often, we become impressed with our own importance and achievements and forget about God.

> *Godliness exalts a nation, but sin is a disgrace to any people.* Ch14 v34

> *The Lord is far from the wicked, but he hears the prayers of the righteous.* Ch15 v29

> *When the ways of people please the Lord, he makes even their enemies live at peace with them.* Ch16 v7

The name of the Lord is a strong fortress; the godly run to him and are safe. Ch18 v10 The godly walk with integrity; blessed are their children after them. Ch20 v7

Whosoever pursues godliness and unfailing love will find life, godliness, and honor. Ch21 v21

The godly are like trees that bear life-giving fruit, and those who save lives are wise. Ch11 v30

If the godly compromise with the wicked, it is like polluting a fountain or muddying a spring. Ch25 v26

When the godly succeed, everyone is glad. When the wicked take charge, people go into hiding. Ch28 v12

STEP 23: CHOICES – OMNISCIENT GOD

This section of Proverb's plan has some great verses. They're a little scary, but great to know. The truth is that God knows what's going on in our lives. We may wonder at times what's happening and why so many bad things are occurring. Despite that, we're assured there's nothing happening that escapes God's notice. He's constantly aware of our actions and also the motives for our actions. He sees into our minds and hearts.

I love what technology has provided for us in so many areas. What once seemed impossible is now common practice. With MRIs, CAT scans and endoscopes we can see into the human body like never before. With infrared technology soldiers can see into the night to view an enemy as clearly as if it were daylight. What's amazing to me is that many of these technologies didn't exist when I was born.

With these advancements in technology it's no longer hard to understand or believe that God can view our inmost structures and thoughts and see our actions in the light or in the dark. What we do, think and feel are all open and viewable to God. Wow! Isn't it great to have God's mercy, forgiveness and grace? Proverbs tells us that we have a future and a hope. God won't turn his back on those who honor him. God provides a future and a hope to those who serve him and they won't be disappointed with that future.

> *The Lord is watching everywhere, keeping his eye on both the evil and the good. Ch15 v3 The Lord's searchlight penetrates the human spirit, exposing every hidden motive.* Ch20 v27

> *People may think they are doing what is right, but the Lord examines the heart. The Lord is more pleased when we do what is just and right than when we give him sacrifices.* Ch21 v2-3

> *Don't envy sinners, but always continue to fear the Lord. For surely you have a future ahead of you; your hope will not be disappointed.* Ch23 v17-18

STEP 24: CHOICES – TRUTH

At one time or another we've all had lies told about us. It hurts when we hear about it and we want to jump right on it and set the record straight. We want the real truth to be shouted out for all to hear. We want to call our friends and let them know that there is no truth to the lies being told. When situations like this happen it makes us feel really bad and we wonder how anyone could be so unfair and unkind.

After I retired from teaching and was elected to the local school board, I began to work very hard to bring about some changes I believed were necessary to improve teaching and learning in the district. Then the attacks began! Stories were made up and vicious lies were told about me. I'd never seen anything like this in all my years of working in education.

During board meetings, people would line up, sometimes twenty-five to thirty deep to howl and scream. I always seemed to be the one singled out for focus of the attacks. I remember writing this Bible verse down on the papers in front of me:

> *Trust in the Lord with all your heart; do not depend*
> *on your own understanding. Seek his will in all you do,*
> *and he will direct your paths.* Ch3 v5-6

I read it over and over again as the attacks continued. This gave me a focus to my responsibilities and allowed me to keep prospective on what was important. These attacks continued not just for months, but for years.

At first, I wanted to answer every critic and every lie. However, I was told by those in the professional political arena to let it go, and let those who wanted to make up lies do so. My advisors said that the truth would eventually come out and my work recognized.

I followed this advice. It cost me some friends, who really weren't friends at all. Friends don't run when the problems come, they pull closer to you to protect and assist you. I let those who wanted to tell lies and to make up stories do so. I did my job as best I could and didn't look back.

Truth will hold up and lies will be exposed. Maybe they won't be exposed quickly, maybe not even in our lifetime. Even so, God has the long view and he'll take care of the truth issues and defend us when questions arise about our honesty. It does hurt and our pride can get in the way, but we need to rely on God to take care of the situation. The truth will eventually win out.

> *Truth stands the test of time; lies are soon exposed.*
> Ch12 v19

STEP 25: CHOICES – HONORING GOD

God blesses everyone on the planet. We've all been blessed in varying amounts physically, financially and materially; yet, that's not the best measure. Health, family, friends, and work are far more important. They are better measurements of our blessings than our bank accounts.

Proverbs reminds us that of the material wealth with which we are blessed, we are to return part of it back to God. Proverbs says God will give back to those who honor him with their giving. He will overflow their barns with grain and their vats with wine. This step in Proverb's plan is to honor God by giving back to him our best fruits of labor and he will reward us in return with blessings far above those we might expect.

To sum up, we can honor God by doing the best job possible in everything we do. We honor God at our job by working hard, being responsible, honest and being the best employee we can be. We must honor the work relationship and be thankful and respectful in our work. When we go to church and worship God we should enter his house respectfully with the deep understanding that he is God and we are his children. We need to enter his house with an attitude of awe, humbleness and humility.

> *Be silent, and know that I am God! I will be honored by every nation. I will be honored throughout the world.* Psalm 46: 10

> *Honor the Lord with your wealth and with the best part of everything your land produces. Then he will fill your barns with grain, and your vats will overflow with the finest wine.* Ch3 v9-10

STEP 26: CHOICES – BEING GODLY

Proverb's plan expresses the advantages of a Godly life. It also expresses some of the consequences of a wicked life. It's clear that living a life of Godliness is full of advantages for the individual and society. Once again, the reality of choices is presented to us. The options are clear and easy to understand. We know that some will disregard this truth to choose a life of wickedness, resulting in instability, failure, and pain. It's important to understand the choice is ours. We constantly make the choices that will determine our destination. We can blame it on others but it doesn't alter the fact that it's our call, our responsibility, our choice.

The earnings of the godly enhance their lives, but evil people squander their money on sin. Ch10 v16

The godly are like trees that bear life giving fruit, and those who save lives are wise. Ch11 v30

Wickedness never brings stability; only the godly have deep roots. Ch12 v3

Godliness helps people all through life, while the evil are destroyed by their wickedness. Ch13 v6

The life of the godly is full of light and joy, but the sinner's light is snuffed out. Ch13 v9

It is better to be poor and godly than rich and dishonest. Ch16 v8

When the godly succeed, everyone is glad. When the wicked take charge, people go into hiding. Ch28 v12

STEP 27: CHOICES – HOPE

Proverbs reveals the importance of hopes and dreams. It's true it's individual hopes and dreams that move the human race forward. Throughout history men and women have dreamed about what could be done on the earth. So many have worked so hard to accomplish the impossible. These people brought progress to the human race. They dreamed dreams and fought to see them come true.

Sometimes it cost the dreamer only his effort and wealth. Other times it cost him his life and fortune. The list of achievements runs through the ages. Hopes and dreams offer mankind a future that is better than the past, a future where there is a reduction in sickness, pain and one where life is extended. God expresses to us the vital importance of individual and collective hope. Nevertheless, regardless of time or century our ultimate hope for the future needs to reside in God. He alone is the author and finisher of our faith.

Hope deferred makes the heart sick, but when dreams come true, there is life and joy. Ch13 v12

It is pleasant to see dreams come true, but fools will not turn from evil to attain them. Ch13 v19

STEP 28: CHOICES – UNDERSTANDING OUR PATH

We begin life with absolutely no understanding of who we are or knowledge of the vast and confusing world around us. The first few years of our life are spent trying to develop intellectual and emotional tools that help us understand our world and ourselves. It takes nearly fifty years to understand and gain perspective on life and its meaning. We struggle as we begin to mature and accumulate enough wisdom to understand our place in the world. Still our understanding is so limited and our clarity of vision is so distorted that we are vastly restricted.

Clearly from Proverb's plan and from our own experience it's only God who fully understands. Only he can understand the ultimate destination of our travels. We see the need for communication with God, through prayer and reading his word, to help us gain wisdom, perspective and direction. Since we are limited in our understanding and perspective, and he is knowledgeable and wise, we need to choose to seek his guidance.

> *How can we understand the road we travel? It is the Lord who directs our steps.* Ch20 v24

STEP 29: CHOICES – PLANNING FOR PARENTS AND CHILDREN ✝

Deciding to bring children into the world and being accountable for rearing them to be responsible adults are two of the most important decisions that a man and a woman can make. Few commitments have as much impact and require as much drive and determination as having and properly rearing children. They are choices that will forever change the whole life of the couple. They aren't decisions that last only during the pregnancy, or even through school age years. Parenting is a job that lasts a lifetime.

In terms of a running analogy, it's a marathon and not a sprint. During a sprint, or short race, the physiological requirements of the run require a physical reaction that is fast and strong. Even so, the race and its requirements are short lived and are soon over. Mistakes involving hydration or nutrition can be overcome because of the short distance of the race.

It isn't true in a marathon. If a runner runs too fast their body may fatigue and might not take them to the finish line. If the pace is too slow with the extra stress and fatigue of a longer race time, the runner may not make it to the finish line. All along the marathon, care must be taken to make sure the runner maintains the correct pace, stays hydrated and takes in sufficient nutrition to sustain the runner's energy requirements. Even with proper training, pacing, hydration and nutrition the marathon seems to go on forever. Energy management is vital with constant attention given to energy intake and expenditure.

So it is with having children and bringing them successfully into adulthood. This rewarding task takes constant thought, planning and endurance. Raising children can't just be put on autopilot and allow the years to run. Just as energy management, nutrition and hydration are important aspects in the running of a marathon, so communication, discipline, love and endurance are among the important items needing constant attention in the rearing of children.

Make no mistake; this is tiring. Time and energy management are vital to successful parenting. The energy of working couples is depleted by the demands of their individual jobs. They're going to come home tired and in need of some rest and relaxation. Yet, the responsibilities of parenting require them to spend quality time in education, communication, guidance, play and accountability. This won't be easy but it's a necessity and will pay large dividends in the education and development of the child.

> *Look straight ahead, and fix your eyes on what lies before you. Mark out a straight path for your feet; then stick to the path and stay safe. Don't get sidetracked; keep your feet from following evil.* Ch4 v25-26

Planning is an important concept discussed in Proverbs. The first step in life's formula is planning itself. Life has always been complicated and the travel through it is difficult and just plain hard. This is important to learn quickly in life. Remember, as I have said before, "Life is hard!" On top of being hard, many times life isn't even fair; so these are two great truths. Therefore, we need to accept it and make plans on how to successfully move through it. Financial and spiritual planning are key components in a successful life plan for parenting.

> *Look straight ahead, and fix your eyes on what lies before you. Mark out a straight path for your feet; then stick to the path and stay safe.* Ch4 v25

> *A prudent person foresees the danger ahead and takes precautions; the simpleton goes blindly on and suffers the consequences.* Ch22 v3 (See also Ch27 v12)

FINANCIAL PLANNING FOR PARENTS

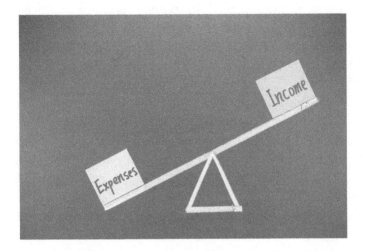

One vital part of the parents' financial plan should include a savings account for their child's future education. Higher education, either an advanced vocational school or college, is both vital and expensive. It's vital because of the need for our citizens to be highly educated and competitive in an international, global arena. Like it or not, our children will be competing internationally for jobs. Our national economy is intertwined with the economies of other countries and we are competing as never before.

It's expensive because the cost of education has risen exponentially. This is a result of upgrading campuses to include better student facilities as well as high technology capabilities in all areas of learning.

Parents should begin saving for their children's education as early as possible. An educational savings account that has tax advantages should be started. Funds that are invested early draw interest and assist in the cost of education.

One way to gain the needed educational funds might be to reduce the number of toys that are purchased at birthdays and Christmas and place money into an educational account. Many parents in our country overindulge their children at birthdays and other holidays. For instance, instead of renting a bounce house, put that money into the child's education fund. Parents could spend half of the normal birthday amount on toys and put the other half in this account. This example is a great one for grandparents and other relatives to follow too. Tell the child what you are doing and stress the importance of education and its cost. By doing this they can begin to understand the sacrifices needed to provide them with a good education.

Parents also need to help the child develop an individualized financial plan for their future. Children need to learn that money is earned by working. So even small children should be given chores around the home. These chores could be cleaning their room, taking out the trash, working in the yard, taking care of a pet, along with dozens of other activities. An allowance should be paid to the child for taking care of these work activities. From the money that's earned the parent needs to instruct the children in tithing and saving. The tax reality will come soon enough, but the parent should help their child understand that ten percent of what they earn should be tithed and given back to God.

Also important is that an additional ten percent should be saved. It could be used for a rainy day fund or for special purchases that are important to the child. For instance, it could be very rewarding for the child to be able to purchase gifts for dad, mom and siblings for birthdays or other special events. This gives the child a personal satisfaction of giving to others and develops in them a sense of power. This power shows some control over their lives and teaches small but important lessons.

To sum up, planning and developing a sound financial direction for the future is one of the most important skills a child can learn. It's taught in Proverbs, but also in every major business or military training program in the world. General Douglas MacArthur once said, "Any plan, no matter how ill conceived is infinitely better than no plan at all."

The parenting process must include instructing the child in developing a mechanism for a continual planning model. This model should include making conscious choices that move their life in a sustained, positive direction.

Spiritual Planning for Parents

Spiritual concern in Proverb's plan is extremely important. From birth through the high school years it's essential to teach a child about God and his word. Start early by reading Bible stories about the great men and women in the Bible. Children's editions are readily available with colorful pictures that can enhance the stories and make their meanings clear. Christian morals and ethics learned from these stories will get a child started in the right direction. It also shows a child that these stories with their moral and ethical lessons are important to the parents.

It's also important for parents to take their children to church for additional Bible study and fellowship with other Christians. Too often they tend to fall down here. They are tired from the workweek and the household chores have piled up. This usually means housework needs to be accomplished on Saturday. This leaves only Sunday to try and sleep in and get some needed rest. Still, it's very important for parents to take their child to church and join them there in fellowship and worship. It's not enough to drop them off at church or to send them with another family. This needs to be a family event where the importance of God in the family's life is displayed by joining together in Bible study and worship. This time spent in the spiritual development of the child is priceless.

Teach your children to choose the right path, and when they are older, they will remain upon it. Ch22 v6

A parent can't wait until junior high or high school. That's too late to make vital spiritual and moral growth. My mother used to say, "You can't put an adult head on the child overnight." It takes years of spiritual education and training to develop into a moral and ethical adult. It's strategic that parents read the Bible to their children and help them memorize and assimilate important verses of faith, courage, security, hope and love that will help them through the difficult times in life.

> *My child, don't lose sight of good planning and insight.*
> *Hang on to them, for they fill you with life and bring honor*
> *and respect.* Ch3 v21

Step 30: Choices – Discipline

Discipline is a significant topic discussed in Proverb's plan. It's a topic that's misunderstood in societies especially in our modern one. However, it's clear in Proverbs that discipline is vital if a child is to develop into a wise and intelligent individual.

> *To learn, you must love discipline; it is stupid to hate correction.* Ch12 v1

The meaning of the word discipline is better understood if we look at its roots. The word has a close relationship to the Latin word for instruction or knowledge. It also has a relationship to the word disciple or being a student. So this implies a connection with instruction, learning or gaining knowledge. These positive characteristics are crucial to an understanding of the word as it applies to parents disciplining their children.

Proverbs reminds us that discipline is a joint responsibility for both the parent and child. It's evident that if parents love their children they should be actively involved in teaching, training, directing, controlling, and instructing their children.

> *If you refuse to discipline your children, it proves that you don't love them; if you love your children, you will be prompt to discipline them.* Ch13 v24

Too often discipline is thought of as punishment. In a broad sense this isn't true. True discipline is so much more. It's much more involved in teaching and training than it is in punishment. Nonetheless, appropriate punishment can play a role.

It's hard to think a parent wouldn't love their child enough to discipline them. Yet, after teaching for over four decades I can assure you that this is true. Over and over again at the high school level, I encountered many students who hadn't been properly disciplined by their parents. This caused situations that were tragic in nature. These students had trouble coping with school. They were constantly in trouble with their teachers, school officials, police officers, and even their peers. They hadn't been given the proper discipline necessary to be well adjusted. Many didn't have an operational skill set that allowed them to be successful in relationships and in modern organizational surroundings.

The discipline of a child isn't easy. Let's be very clear here, the discipline of a child is hard. It requires that a parent be on duty 24/7 to guide, correct, encourage, teach and model while being ready to forgive and patiently move on to a new day.

Parents may want to give up at times in the struggle to discipline their children. They must never do so. Disciplining is very difficult and requires remarkable consistency to be done well. It's imperative to continue with the struggle and never give up the fight. They may get discouraged, frustrated, and at times feel like the effort is two steps forward combined with one to two steps back. It's vital that the parents never, ever give up. The outcome is too important and the results will ultimately be worth the effort.

Teach your children to choose the right path, and when they are older, they will remain on it. Ch22 v6

This is a great promise from God. If parents take the time and effort to discipline and teach their children the proper path, God promises that once on that path, the child will remain on it. This doesn't mean children won't make mistakes or take an incorrect turn now and again. After all, they're human and making perfect decisions concerning our lives is just not in our genes. So, the promise in Proverbs is, even if children take a number of detours, they will ultimately return to the correct and proper pathway.

Discipline your children, and they will give you happiness and peace of mind. Ch29 v17

Over the years, I have experienced many unhappy parent/teacher meetings in a school setting. These usually concerned the undisciplined behavior of their child with its consequences. Most parents realized they needed help to resolve numerous problems resulting from their child's lack of proper conduct and discipline. Many of them were at their wits end and didn't know what to do. They hadn't been properly disciplined and trained themselves and now they were lost. The predictable results were that both the parent and the child were unhappy with the situation. There was little or no peace at home and a dim hope for a productive future for the child or the parent.

Discipline your children while there is hope. If you don't, you will ruin their lives. Ch19 v18

To discipline and reprimand a child produces wisdom, but a mother is disgraced by an undisciplined child. Ch29 v15

In too many of these school meetings I observed mothers who were disgraced and embarrassed by the behaviors and attitudes of their children. Unfortunately, many of these meetings were with high school age students. Proverbs promises that if we train a child correctly when they are young then when they are older they will not depart the proper path. Proverbs promises that over time the child will realize that the early training was important. The cold, hard fact is that if discipline is to make a life long difference, it must begin when the child is young.

I've heard many excuses why a parent wasn't properly disciplining their children. I learned long ago that for many people any excuse is a good excuse, but it doesn't change the facts. Disciplining an individual is hard, consistent work that takes years and must begin early in the life of the child. It's there that one's best chance for success is found. Train, teach, instruct, and control children when they are young. This is when they want to hear from you and need to hear from you, then, when they're older they'll remember your love, concern and teaching.

A certain danger in delaying the discipline of children is that the child will become the man. The way the child behaves today will determine who they ultimately become.

> *Even children are known by the way they act, whether their conduct is pure and right.* Ch20 v11

Children develop reputations that follow them throughout school and into their adult lives. This standing may at times become a self-fulfilling prophecy of who they become. Care must be taken that this reputation is thoughtfully developed and that the self-fulfilling prophecy is positive.

It's true that parents have the responsibility to discipline the child, but the child has the responsibility to learn from the parents. This is clear in Proverb's plan.

> *Only a fool despises a parent's discipline; whoever learns from correction is wise.* Ch16 v5

> *To learn, you must love discipline; it is stupid to hate correction.* Ch12 v1

> *...a wise person learns from instruction.* Ch21 v11

> *Listen my child to what your father teaches you, don't neglect your mother's teaching. What you learn from them will crown you with grace and clothe you with honor.* Ch1 v8-9

This process involves a partnership between the parent and the child. Having said that, it must be understood that the parent is the senior partner. Parents aren't perfect and raising a child in a disciplined and loving way is very difficult. Still, with all their faults the parent must be the one to take on the responsibility of guiding, educating and disciplining. The parent needs to be the adult in the relationship, not just a friend, and have confidence they will provide exactly what is needed to bring up the child. There can be no quarter given in this. The parent must make the tough choices that are needed to discipline and guide the child. Remember however, that discipline is a teaching and training process. Through it, the child will become able to make their own choices and to take responsibility for their own life.

What's clear from Proverbs is that a child's heart and mind are immature and foolish. Discipline is needed to move away from immaturity and foolishness and move in the direction of maturity and wisdom.

A youngster's heart is filled with foolishness, but physical discipline will drive it far away. Ch22 v15

Don't fail to correct your children. They won't die if you spank them. Physical discipline may well save them from death. Ch22 v13

In our modern era, spanking a child is frowned upon. Some individuals view it as a form of child abuse and worthy of a referral to Child Protective Services. This is an extreme position in a world that's desperately trying to find its way. Proverbs is clear, physical discipline has a place in the training of a child. Despite that, it shouldn't be overdone nor should it be the primary method of discipline. It's a tool, just one tool that can be effective under certain circumstances. Some children don't respond to physical correction in a worthwhile way, while others do. Using physical discipline should be limited and it should never be severe.

Physical discipline should never be used when the parent is angry or emotionally upset. Parents are cautioned to be thoughtful when choosing physical discipline. All other possible options for correction of the child need to be considered and the best course of action needs to be utilized.

The child could be brought into a brief discussion about the situation and given the opportunity to come up with a corrective course of action for their behavior. If possible, a solution should be found that is agreed upon by both the parent and the child. If not, the parent is the mature one and should develop a corrective plan that teaches and trains the child to be more responsible.

> *Physical punishment cleanses away evil; such discipline purifies the heart.* Ch20 v30

> *My Child, don't ignore it when the Lord disciplines you, and don't be discouraged when he corrects you. For the Lord corrects those he loves, just as a father corrects a child in whom he delights.* Ch3 v11

STEP 31: CHOICES – TROUBLE IN OUR FAMILY

✝

Those who bring trouble on their families inherit only the wind. Ch11 v29

We've all seen families in trouble. As a teacher, I saw it over and over again with my students. When parents act irresponsibly in some aspect of their lives the consequences are always seen and felt in their families. The use and abuse of alcohol, drugs, unfaithfulness, overworking, or financial irresponsibility are just a few of the things that can destroy a family. It just can't be overstated how important the parents and their behaviors are in the family relationships. Family members see everything that's going on within the family structure. This will influence who they are and what they will become. Values obtained by children are caught as well as taught.

It won't work to say to children, "Do as I say and not as I do." Kids aren't designed to learn that way. They look up to their parents and develop their life view while watching them. If they choose to act in irresponsible ways then their children will more than likely develop the same bad behaviors.

Parents have a huge responsibility to children to get it right. Bringing children into the world accompanies with it the greatest obligation to live lives in responsible and healthy ways for the well being of their children. If parents choose to sow the wind, they will surely inherit the whirlwind.

STEP 32: CHOICES – CHILDREN ARE KNOWN BY THEIR ACTS

Even children are known by the way they act, whether their conduct is pure and right. Ch20 v11

It's hard for many parents to accept and deal with this truth. Basically what you see in a child's consistent behavior is what you will see in the adult. There are behaviors that are common and normal in a child that they will outgrow as they mature. For example, I never saw a high school student still using a pacifier. What I am talking about are behaviors that include temper tantrums, hitting, biting, screaming, kicking and other disrespectful actions and attitudes.

At first they may seem cute. A mother may look at her child and say something like "Isn't she cute, she's so stubborn, what am I going to do with her? I just can't control her. I can't wait until she can go to school." Another parent may say, "Look at Johnny, he's so headstrong. He kicks his brothers and sister when he doesn't get his way. I keep talking to his father about it but nothing seems to change." Parents need to remember that the child will become the adult and that bad behaviors that aren't corrected in childhood will continue to be problems in their adult life, and the consequences of these bad behaviors will be more severe. Spoiled adult behaviors lead to the loss of a job, a troubled marriage or other social problems.

Proverbs has it right, *Even children are known by the way they act.* This gives us a clue about how a child will be known as an adult. Of course it's by his actions, deeds that resulted from the education, discipline, teaching and love that came from the parents. In sad cases, the lack of such parenting is an adult who's just a larger version of a spoiled, undisciplined, and uncontrolled child. This results in a tragedy!

To keep this from becoming a reality parents should follow the truths found in Proverbs. The first step is to develop a discipline or behavior plan. Remember that Proverbs is really big on planning. The parent shouldn't just let things happen, but should look ahead, watch what's going on and make a plan. In this case make a behavior plan for the child. What behaviors do you want to see reinforced and which ones do you want to see changed or gone? Decide what your limits are going to be in regard to the child's behaviors. Recognize that children, just like adults, will test the limits of the plan.

I know you are shocked at this; but think of the way you acted growing up. You need to be ready for this and decide beforehand what the limits will be. Then you must take action to change unwanted behaviors. For example, if your child refuses to follow your verbal direction, do you warn the child once, twice, three times or just keep warning them until you have no credibility on the issue.

I tend to like the three strikes rule, like in baseball. Warn the child once what needs to be done. Strike one! If the child gives no correct response, then strike two. Give another corrective warning. If the child responds correctly, then all is well. If the child continues to resist and won't follow simple and clear corrective guidance, strike three! Then, there needs to be a price paid by the child. This could be a time out, the loss of the use of a toy, or no dessert after dinner. There's an important principle here, the child should know the plan. They could help choose a reasonable outcome for breaking the plan. They should receive the results or consequences of their choices. They can choose to comply or accept the consequences of their actions. It's their responsibility.

There are several things to keep in mind during this process. First develop a plan and second follow the plan without exception. Always be consistent! Don't ever give up nor allow yourself to repeat over and over again, "The next time you do that…" Just follow through! You must be 100 percent consistent and follow your plan, whatever rules you set in motion. You must always follow the plan exactly, just like clockwork. The child deserves, and needs to believe, that your behavior and actions will be solid and predictable. The child may or may not like your plan. Even so, eventually they will appreciate it and will especially respect your consistency, believability, and your love.

There are so many behaviors that are expressed by children and even adults in our modern society that are destructive. Small, but important things that if corrected during childhood will make them better employees, parents, and teachers. These include using the English language properly, not using profanity, not expressing negative attitudes or a lack of respect for adults.

A term that's used a lot in our society today expresses this lack of proper training and conduct. The term is "Whatever!" The young and old alike express it, "Whatever dude!" can be heard over and over again in modern conversations. However, what's lost in the message is that "Whatever!" isn't good enough. It never has been and it never will be. This implies that sloppiness or carelessness in our conversations and work habits are normal and fine. Nothing could be further from the truth. Our work place and our personal relationships suffer when we are shoddy and lazy in our approach to our lives and work. This needs to be corrected and it must start with our children and their early education and training.

There is so much truth to this ancient saying concerning attention to detail and getting it right. A small overlooked circumstance or shoddy work can have devastating results.

> For the want of a nail the shoe was lost;
> For the want of a shoe the horse was lost;
> For the want of a horse the rider was lost;
> For the want of a rider the battle was lost;
> For loss of the battle the kingdom was lost.
> Unknown

Teach your children to choose the right path, and when they are older, they will remain upon it. Ch22 v6

A youngster's heart is filled with foolishness, but discipline will drive it away. Ch22 v15

I have loved this verse all my life and have depended on it for many, many years; *Teach your children to choose the right path,...* It's one of God's promises that has sustained many parents through tough, disturbing times with their own children. Being a parent is very hard, and we only have one chance to get it right. Being human, we as parents will make many, many mistakes. Proverbs tells us that what we do in love will bear a love response, but waiting for that mature love response from our children can take years and a lot of holding on to the promise, ...*when they are older, they will remain on it.*

There were many times my wife and I would pray, "How much older do they have to become?" Don't get me wrong we have two wonderful sons who have awesome families. Of course our grandchildren are the smartest and the cutest in the world. We love them all and they've been great to my wife and me. They're fantastic examples of good choices in one's life. Yet they, like all the rest of us, are human. They have made mistakes, we all have. While they were trying their wings and leaving the nest we watched them flutter and fall from one branch of life's tree to another. It hurts to watch this happen but it's both normal and necessary.

My wife and I claimed this verse, *Train up a child in the way he should go: and when he is old, he will not depart from it. (KJV)* I really can't tell you the number of times that we reminded God of his promise as we worried ourselves to sleep. At times we agonized, trying to trust that God would be faithful and bring them through their struggles. We never doubted God's promise as being true, but we did struggle with God's path and his timing. Thank God he is so faithful!

STEP 33: CHOICES – EDUCATION AND INSTRUCTION

Instruction and education of the child is a very important concept in Proverb's plan.

> *Commit yourself to instruction; attune your ears to hear words of knowledge.* Ch23 v12

> *...a wise person learns from instruction.* Ch21 v11

> *Follow my advice, my son; always treasure my commands. Obey them and live! Guard my teachings as your most precious possession. Tie them on your fingers as a reminder. Write them deep within your heart.* Ch7 v1-3

There's no doubt that Solomon understood a couple of things that are very important. One is the fact that adults, or older individuals, have more knowledge and experience than the young. With that experience they have made a number of mistakes. If they are wise, the knowledge gained from their consequences may very well have taught them valuable lessons. Adults can teach the young about their bad decisions and the hurt and pain that came from them. What a wonderful learning environment for instruction and learning to take place. A person who has learned practical lessons from real life events is a great resource for others who are just beginning their search for life's answers.

Too often today in a formal learning environment the student and the teacher are believed to be on equal footing. Such isn't the case. It's believed by many that the teacher is to be a guide to the student but not to take a vital instructional role in the education process. This isn't the view expressed in Proverbs. Adults have gained more experience and knowledge from life and have a proper role teaching about that experience.

> *If you listen to constructive criticism, you will be at home among the wise.* Ch15 v31

> *If you reject criticism, you only harm yourself, but if you listen to correction, you will grow in understanding.* Ch15 v32

Some individuals accept instruction easily and others reject it. Proverbs gives us a warning concerning this.

> *Whoever stubbornly refuses to accept criticism will suddenly be broken beyond repair.* Ch29 v1

> *Carry out my instructions; don't forsake them. Guard them, for they will lead you to a fulfilled life.* Ch4 v13

Stated in Proverb's plan is there's an important, if not vital, connection between the parent and the child in regard to instruction and learning. There's a directive that parents need to be involved in the instruction of the child. The parent is to teach the child in all areas of life. This role can't be given over to anyone else. Education of the child is the direct responsibility of the parent. I don't mean to infer that the child has no culpability. In fact, Proverbs makes it very clear that the child does have responsibility in the learning process. The child is told to:

> *Listen to your father's instruction...* Ch4 v1

> *Carry out my instructions; don't forsake them. Guard them, for they will lead you to a fulfilled life.* Ch4 v13

> *My son, obey your father's commands, and don't neglect your mother's teaching. For these commands and this teaching are a lamp to light the way ahead of you. The correction of discipline is the way to life.* Ch6 v 20-23

> *Follow my advice, my son; always treasure my commands. Obey them and live! Guard my teachings as your most precious possession. Tie them on your fingers as a reminder. Write them deep within your heart.* Ch7 v1-4

One of the problems of our society is the concept that children don't need to listen to their parents, grandparents and teachers. Society would have our children believe that they are just as smart and wise as their adult caretakers so there is no need to learn from this older group. The thought is that the older generation doesn't understand the newer generation and their problems. The belief is everything is changing so rapidly that the older group doesn't get it.

The reality is that human conditions aren't changing. The problems of humans working and living together and becoming educated and wise are still the same old problems. They may be wrapped up in different packages and called by different names, but the issues of life are still the same as they have always been and we need wisdom and understanding to deal with them. This is exactly where the older group can provide instruction and wisdom to help the young understand and cope with modern problems. Just the ability to use an iPad, play video games, watch MTV or tune into a reality TV show doesn't qualify as being wise.

I really don't know how our culture came up with this idea of the young and immature having superior wisdom, judgment, and understanding compared to their seniors. I don't know of a single culture in history that has embraced this idea. Be that as it may, it's just plain silly and we need to understand that if the young are to become wise and gain understanding in how to govern their lives, they must learn it from the instruction and wisdom of their parents, grandparents, teachers, and pastors.

Yet, there are those who resist or reject instruction and any constructive criticism. For these individuals Solomon assigns the name fool. He was clear that they aren't worthy of the effort being wasted on them.

> *Don't waste your breath on fools, for they will despise the wisest of advice.* Ch23 v9

A major point about instruction and learning that's expressed in Proverbs is that learning needs to be a joy, not so much in the fun sense but in the expression of joy that comes from learning relevant things. These pertinent things should be taught in meaningful and organized ways. Once again, it's plain that the early and consistent education of a child is important.

> *The wise are known for their understanding and instruction is appreciated if it's well presented.* Ch16 v21

Step 34: Choices – Long Life

Most individuals want a good, long, productive life. Much of our efforts throughout life are focused on trying to gain and maintain our physical and mental health. Proverb's plan speaks to this point directly and with assurance; the fear and awe of God is a major contributor to our health and length of life.

> *Fear of the Lord lengthens one's life, but the years of the wicked are cut short.* Ch10 v27

> *Godly people find life; evil people find death.* Ch11 v19

> *My Child never forget the things I have taught you. Store my commands in your heart for they will give you a long and satisfying life.* Ch3 v1

> *My Child, listen to me and do as I say, and you will have a long, good life.* Ch4 v10

A good, long, life is promised if we place God in his proper role and follow his commands. Parents have the responsibility to teach their children about God and to lead them to a proper relationship with him. The child needs to take advantage of this teaching and instruction by the parents. This leads to learning about God's principles and commandments. Both common sense and wisdom are by-products of learning about God, inviting him into our lives and following his commandments and principles.

> *The person who strays from common sense will end up in the company of the dead.* Ch21 v16

The way of the Godly leads to life; their path does not lead to death. Ch12 v28

In the same way wisdom is sweet to your soul. If you find it, you will have a bright future, and your hope will not be cut short. Ch24 v14

This plan presented in Proverbs isn't new. It's a recurring theme. Parents who bring children into the world have a God given responsibility to teach them about God and his ways. Children are to listen and learn the great truths that are taught by their parents. Proverbs makes this divine partnership very clear. When parents take this role seriously and commit themselves to teach their children about God, it's a wonderful thing. By taking their children to church, Bible study, Vacation Bible School, youth camps, and other church related events, parents show the respect and commitment they have to raising their children in the fear and admonition of God. It will pay huge dividends in the life of the children. I have seen throughout my life that parents who take the time to educate their children in the teaching and understanding of God, see the fruits of their labor rewarded.

In addition to showing wisdom and providing joy to ones parents by listening to them and learning from them, is the fact that doing so is a matter of life and death. One of the Ten Commandments states that if one honors their father and mother then their days upon the earth will be long. (Exodus 20: 12) Proverbs backs up this promise by stating that if a child doesn't listen to their parents and dishonors them then the child's life will be cut short.

If you curse your father or mother, the lamp of your life will be snuffed out. Ch20 v20

Listen, my child, to what your father teaches you. Don't neglect your mother's teaching. What you learn from them will crown you with grace and clothe you with honor. Ch1 v8

My child, never forget the things I have taught you. My children listen to me. Listen to your father's instruction.

Pay attention and grow wise, for I am giving you good guidance. Don't turn away from my teaching. Ch3 v1-2

My child, listen to me and do as I say, and you will have a long, good life. Ch4 v10

My son, obey your father's commands, and don't neglect your mother's teaching. For these commands and this teaching are a lamp to light the way ahead of you. The correction of discipline is the way to life. Ch6 v20 & 23

Follow my advice, my son; always treasure my commands. Obey them and live. Guard my teachings as your most precious possession. Ch7 v1-2

A wise child brings joy to a father; a foolish child brings grief to a mother. Ch10 v1

Children who mistreat their father or chase away their mother are a public disgrace and an embarrassment. Ch19 v26

STEP 35: CHOICES – AVOIDING EVIL IN THE WORLD

It's a common belief in our modern world that evil doesn't exist. This popular thought holds that the problems that we find in the human condition are caused by influences of poverty; educational inequality; environmental influences; fate; bad luck; living outside the vortex zone; or just being dealt a bad hand. An active force of evil isn't even considered because it's believed to be only a superstition, an anti-intellectual viewpoint or a holdover from a time when uninformed man embraced a now out of date religious position.

Throughout the Bible and in Proverb's plan, God holds a different position. This view is there is an evil force in the world and it's to be avoided and resisted at all costs. There are many references in both the Old and New Testaments that tell more of the role of evil in the world and people who are influenced by it.

> *Stay alert! Watch out for your great enemy, the devil. He prowls around like a roaring lion, looking for someone to devour.* I Peter 5: 8

> *Don't envy evil people; don't desire their company. For they spend their days plotting violence, and their words are always stirring up trouble.* Ch24 v1-2

There's evil in the world that's trying to make the world a tough place in which to live. People influenced by this force are constantly plotting violence and stirring up trouble. One doesn't have to go much further than a daily newspaper, news website or a radio news program to confirm that there's constant violence and trouble in our communities, states, and nations throughout the world. We shouldn't be surprised at this situation. We've been warned about it in the Bible for a very long time. Proverbs warned us hundreds of years before the life of Christ.

> *Here's a description of worthless and wicked people: They are constant liars signaling their true intentions to their friends by making signs with their eyes and feet and fingers. Their perverted hearts plot evil. They stir up trouble constantly. But they will be destroyed suddenly, broken beyond all hope or healing.* Ch6 v12-15

Proverbs tells us that not only is there evil in the world, but people influenced by it are going to try and harm others. Evil disguises itself in various camouflaged formats. Usually it's robed as goodness and light. It's advertised as the coolest, most modern and progressive thing. Cigarettes, beer, wine and liquor are shown at the center of family outings, parties with attractive young people, and with old friends sitting together at a local pub. It's seen in the movies coming out of Hollywood; movies full of glamorized violence, graphic and immoral sex, dishonesty and infidelity. It's in newspapers that report stories of a person who stops on the road pretending to help stranded motorists then robs and murders them. The stories go on and on.

> *People with hate in their hearts may sound pleasant enough, but don't believe them. Though they pretend to be kind, their hearts are full of all kinds of evil. While their hatred may be concealed by trickery, it will finally come to light for all to see.* Ch26 v24-26

The great news is that we have been forewarned about evil and the form it takes. It isn't going to have a sign strapped on it saying, "I am evil, stay away I will hurt you, your family and ultimately ruin your entire life." No, it's going to sound good, be inviting, and the latest thing. It's going to look cool, and present itself as the way of the young, the modern, the future. Yet, if we're seeking wisdom, according to Proverb's plan, we'll be better able to see the lies and the deception of evil. We're told with assurance that the hatred of evil will finally come to light for all to see.

If we fall for the deception of evil and become a party to it, we'll suffer along with others who have fallen for the trickery. Once again it's our choice! We need to make wise Godly choices in our lives that keep us away from evil. When all of the evil and hatred finally come into the open we don't want to be counted with those who fell for the deception and thankfully we don't have to be.

We're told how we're to act in the presence of evil and wicked people.

> *Do not envy violent people; don't copy their ways. Such wicked people are an abomination to the Lord, but he offers his friendship to the godly.* Ch3 v31-32

> *The curse of the Lord is on the house of the wicked, but his blessing is on the home of the upright.* Ch3 v33

I guess it could be clearer, but I don't really know how. The behaviors of evil, wicked, violent people are an abomination to God. There's a curse from God on them and their outcomes in life aren't going to be good. On the other hand, God tells us in Proverbs that the opposite is true for those who choose to gain wisdom and live their lives in upright and honest ways. They'll be blessed by God and have a friendship with him. It just doesn't get a whole lot better than that.

A major promise given to us in Proverbs is that we'll be guided throughout our life by Godly conduct.

> *Good people are guided by their honesty; the wicked fall beneath their load of sin.* Ch11 v3

> *Evil people don't understand justice, but those who follow the Lord understand completely.* Ch28 v5

Another major point needs to be made concerning evil people. We need to underscore what the end will be for them in our communities and in our nation. They have no future and their light will be snuffed out. What a powerful statement from God. Those who continually choose to practice evil, violence and harm others will have no future. It doesn't say their light will grow dim, or burn out over time, Proverbs says it will be snuffed out! That means the lives of evil people will be short lived.

God is the opposite of evil; he is loving and just. He hates evil and is against its influence in the world. Wise people choose to live their lives following God's loving plan.

> *Do not fret because of evildoers; don't envy the wicked.*
> *For the evil have no future; their light will be snuffed out.*
> Ch24 v19-20

STEP 36: CHOICES – BECOMING A FOOL

Stay away from fools, for you won't find knowledge there. Ch14 v7

Fools make fun of guilt, but the godly acknowledge it and seek reconciliation. Ch14 v9 *Don't waste your breath on fools, for they will despise the wisest advice.* Ch23 v9

Make no mistake about it, there are fools in the world. If this weren't so, God wouldn't have spent a great deal of time and trouble warning us about them.

A foolish person is thought of as empty headed, or as a person acting unwise or imprudently. If someone chooses to drink too much alcohol at a bar and gets on a bicycle to ride home, weaving carelessly back and forth through streets crowded with moving cars, such a person would be acting the fool and running a great risk of hurting himself.

On the other hand, if this foolish person left the bar and chose to drive home in a car, weaving through crowded streets, he risks not only hurting himself but also hurting others. Foolish people usually end up, not only hurting themselves, but hurting or killing others.

We find fools everywhere in our society, not just on our roads. We find them at our place of work, where we shop, in schools, in our churches, and even in our families. Playing the fool by making bad personal choices can have a variety of consequences. Some of them can be minor while many of them can have disastrous results that can change lives forever. Choosing to play the fool is hardly ever funny and usually has consequences that we wish we had avoided.

Proverbs tells us that having a fool for a son or daughter has serious consequences for the parents.

> *It is painful to be the parent of a fool; there is no joy for the father of a rebel.* Ch17 v21

> *A foolish child brings grief to a father and bitterness to a mother.* Ch17 v25

> *A foolish child is a calamity to a father...* Ch19 v13a

This warning should give us great pause. Words such as painful, no joy, grief, bitterness, and calamity are all used to describe the impact of a foolish child to parents. As we have learned, Proverb's plan gives many suggestions to keep this from happening. This involves both a Godly parent teaching his children about God and his wisdom, and the children listening. It means teaching the child to know God and to have a personal, loving relationship with him. This takes effort on the part of the parent; however, it's one of those things in life that involves a great truth, pay it now, or pay it later. Often paying later involves a higher price and the increased chance of a broken and painful life.

The way to avoid having a fool for a child is to stop it from happening before it gets started. Playing the catch up game is a bad option. Remember the verse:

> *Teach your children to choose the right path, and when they are older, they will remain upon it.* Ch22 v6

This verse provides a big clue on how parents are to train, teach and instruct their children. It just can't be done any other way. We can never be truly successful patching people up. Sure we can try to bring our loved ones back from a foolish lifestyle, but its very hard and almost never fully successful. The time to train is early in the child's life when they are open, willing and in need of direction and instruction. If this door of opportunity for Godly education and training is missed and a foolish lifestyle is established, it's difficult to correct.

Fools have no interest in understanding; they only want to air their own opinions. Ch17 v2

Don't waste your breath on fools, for they will despise the wisest advice. Ch23 v9

You cannot separate fools from their foolishness, even though you grind them like grain with mortar and pestle. Ch27 v22

This paints a very grim picture of the chances of being successful in bringing a fool out of a foolish lifestyle. It's much like trying to bring a person back to a healthy condition after they have spent years eating the wrong foods, being sedentary, drinking too much alcohol, or smoking. After years of these activities multiple physical conditions are likely to develop. These might include heart, lung, and liver diseases. They will probably include weight problems. The consequences of these lifestyles are clear. It may be impossible to come back to a healthy condition. The time to develop a life of wisdom, principled action, and a healthy lifestyle is early in life.

The last consequence of foolish behavior brought out in Proverbs is a tragic one. *People ruin their lives by their own foolishness and then are angry at the Lord.* Ch19 v3

What a tragedy! People ruin their lives because they don't choose to follow Biblical teachings that express God's way of living. Then when things go badly, they won't take the responsibility for the consequences but rather blame God. Of course this just makes the situation worse. God isn't responsible for the bad choices we make in our lives. We are responsible for all of our choices both good and bad. Proverb's plan is full of warnings and directions for our lives that involve our choices. The choices are ours. God isn't willing that bad things happen to us. Too often it seems that we'll have it no other way and choose to express it by our foolish behavior. God would have us choose to be wise and live in a thriving relationship with him.

STEP 37: CHOICES – ALCOHOL AND WINE

Like all harmful moral choices, alcohol use and abuse can have very serious consequences. I've had discussions, including disagreements, with my own family members concerning this. As a young person I experienced some of the outcomes of the use and abuse of alcohol and its effects on family and friends. I determined then that I would never use or even have alcoholic drinks in my home. I've seen my extended family torn by the effects of its use. I'm not sorry that over the years I have taken a stand against it.

Wine produces mockers; liquor leads to brawls.
Whoever is led astray by drink cannot be wise. Ch20 v1

Rulers should not crave liquor. For if they drink, they may forget their duties and be unable to give justice to those who are oppressed. Liquor is for the dying, and wine for those in deep depression. Let them drink to forget their poverty and remember their troubles no more. Ch31 v4-7

It seems that the warnings concerning the use of wine and liquor are apparent. Its use isn't a good thing and is full of real dangers. The choice not to use alcohol relates to developing wisdom in our lives. It isn't an easy thing to do and it will, at times, go against the common and accepted practices of society. When an individual is twenty-one years of age does he/she have the right to use alcohol? Of course they have the legal right, but does that make it the right thing to do? Even more importantly, does it lead to the development of the person of wisdom described in Proverb's plan?

Remember, wisdom cries in the streets calling for those who would be wise. Many will choose not to listen or heed that call from her. They want to develop their independence and act within their own strong will. Nevertheless, they also need to be careful to make choices that point their lives in the best direction. We all need to make choices that will build a healthy, productive and fulfilling life.

The choice to use alcohol is a trap that costs much yet delivers little. Unfortunately that price is many times too high. These costs too often result in injured bodies and minds, broken families and relationships, and the death or the loss of a truly wise person.

In my role as an educator I have seen the results of fetal alcohol syndrome, teenage alcoholism, student traffic deaths involving alcohol, as well as families torn apart by alcoholism. The wise choice in our lives is to avoid the use of alcohol, and parents would be wise to lead their children by example to avoid its use.

PERSONAL STORY 3

A Future Lost

I taught biology at our local high school. It was late in the school year with only about a month left until graduation. It's such an exciting time for the students, parents and teachers. It's always so much fun and rewarding talking with each of the future graduates about their plans. Some have very organized and thoughtful plans for college or military life while others see graduation from high school as their ultimate goal and have no real idea of what may come next.

It was my custom to take a little extra time on Fridays to walk around the class and talk with students about their future goals. My attention was soon focused on Candice. She was a very smart person who ranked very high academically in her class. She was a hard working student who had a part time job that enabled her to earn some money. Her parents weren't very well off financially so the extra money that Candice was able to bring in was a big help.

I approached Candice and asked her what her plans were for after graduation. She immediately began to tell the story of her future. She said she planned to go to college, not a big school at first but a community college. There she planned to get her general education requirement out of the way. Upon completing her AA degree her plans were to move to a four-year school and complete her bachelor's degree.

Candice continued to discuss her future goals. They included getting a good paying job, finding a boy friend, getting married and then starting a family. She also talked about traveling. She said she had taken German and would love to visit Germany and try out her language skills among the German people.

We then talked about graduation day and what her plans were with family and friends. She told how proud her parents were of her as she was the only one in her family to have completed high school. So out of town family members would be coming to celebrate this huge event. We chatted a few more minutes and I wished her a wonderful weekend as the bell signaled the end of class.

I completed the school day and was glad to see the end of a long and stressful week. I collected the school material that I would need to take home to get ready for the next Monday and a new week.

My family had our usual Friday night events. We rented a movie that the boys wanted to watch, stopped by the local pizza place and picked up a couple of large deep-dish cheese and pepperoni pizzas. The evening went well and soon the boys, my wife and I retired for the evening.

The next morning I went outside and picked up the newspaper. When I opened up to the front page I was shocked. There on the top line was a report of a fatal car accident that involved a drunk driver that took the lives of two high school students. I held my breath as I searched for the names of the students. I rapidly found the names of Candice and one of her friends. Tears filled my eyes as I remembered Candice's hopes and dreams that she had expressed to me just hours before. My heart went out to her parents who must be hurting beyond belief. Two lives full of hope and promise were gone forever.

I could hardly breathe! Anger overcame me as I thought of the selfish, thoughtless man who had dulled his senses with alcohol and then drove to extinguish two lives.

I still drive by the site of the accident. I think of Candice and what her life might have been. I muse how life is so precious yet so fragile. A bad choice by another, as in the abuse of alcohol and then driving a car, can have eternal effects.

STEP 38: CHOICES – HONESTY

Choosing to be honest is vital. In fact, one can't have a good, full and productive life without it. It's important in our family relationships, education, jobs, business and all other aspects of our life. God commands us to be honest and have integrity in all of our dealings with others and in our relationship with him. Honesty is something that parents have to instill in the lives of their children early and with consistency. There is a big pay-off for the children.

When the instruction of honesty and integrity begins at a very basic level it builds as the child grows and develops. It must be taught on a verbal level, but it's vital that it be expressed in parents' behaviors. It won't be effective for the parent to say, "Do as I say, not as I do." The instruction must be coupled by the interaction of the parent with others in an honest and ethical way. Like so many values that are established in life, values of honesty and integrity are caught as well as taught.

> *Follow the steps of good men instead, and stay on the paths of the righteous. For only the upright will live in the land, and those who have integrity will remain in it.* Ch2 v20-21

> *People with integrity have firm footing but those who follow crooked paths will slip and fall.* Ch10 v9

> *The honest will be rescued from harm, but those who are crooked will be destroyed.* Ch28 v18

God promises that if we choose to act with righteousness and integrity, we'll build a life supported by firm footing. God want us to understand how important honesty and integrity are in human relationships. No basic human interaction can stand the test of time if it isn't built on this foundation. When this individual relationship is written large it becomes the backbone for society itself. Without it the whole society is in jeopardy of falling into corruption, decay and failure.

If the godly compromise with the wicked, it is like polluting a fountain or muddying a spring. Ch25 v26

Proverbs tells us that the values of honesty and integrity must never be compromised. This is a hard lesson to learn in our present day of seeking to get along, work it out, make it happen, be tolerant, or be a team player. However, what God is telling us is that there is a right and a wrong. There is a good and an evil. There is the truth and the lie and they can't be reconciled. They are opposites and one will corrupt the other.

A polluted life will result from the mixture of truth and lies in our choices. There can't be a bargain between good and evil or right and wrong. They are polar opposites that can't be reconciled. It may seem wise to choose to live in the gray areas of life. Yet, to operate on the border of right and wrong or good and evil has no future in God's plan.

It seems at times, as we live our lives and teach our children to behave in honest ways, we are losing the battle. There is so much corruption, greed, dishonesty and injustice in our society it appears that evil is winning and honest behavior is losing. It may appear that way on the surface, but that's not really the case.

Do not fret because of evildoers; don't envy the wicked. For the evil have no future; their light will be snuffed out. Ch24 v19-20

The honest will be rescued from harm, but those who are crooked will be destroyed. Ch28 v18

Choosing honest behavior and living a life based on God's truth and moral laws will provide a bright future. In the daily struggle to live in a world so influenced by evil there will be times that a moral battle will be lost. However, the loss of a battle doesn't mean that we have lost the war. Making a mistake hurts and stings but it can be overcome. God's people must work hard to choose to behave in honest ways while operating from a foundation of integrity. It has an impact for the person and for society. It promotes a long and happy life.

> *Fear of the Lord lengthens one's life, but the years of the wicked are cut short.* Ch10 v27 *The hopes of the godly result in happiness, but the expectations of the wicked are all in vain.* Ch10 v28

> *The Lord protects the upright but destroys the wicked.* Ch10 v29

God also tells us in Proverbs how wonderful and powerful a life lived in an honest and truthful way will be.

> *The way of the righteous is like the first gleam of dawn, which shines ever brighter until the full light of day.* Ch4 v18

Righteousness has a vital impact on our lives and on society. It provides the light and promise for a new, brighter and better day. Righteousness is the hope of the present and the future of our world. It begins with the education and training of our children. They must be taught the value of making choices that build honesty and righteousness into their lives. That's the responsibility of the parent and it's the most important job that a parent can perform.

> *Teach your children to choose the right path, and when they are older, they will remain on it.* Ch22 v6

Teachers are hired to teach! That's their primary job. However, teachers and parents know that they are asked to do numerous things in addition to teaching. They are requested at times to act in the role of doctor, nurse, counselor, psychologist, social worker, priest, and parent. So, even though the teacher's primary job is to provide information, train and build skills, it must be understood that they have tremendous influence on the social development of students.

Yet, in reality this can be said about all of us. Each of us holds great power to influence others, both in positive or negative ways. We must take this responsibility very seriously!

PERSONAL STORY 4

Your Impact on Others

I taught biology and physical science at a continuation high school. A continuation high school is designed for those students who have had difficulty being successful in the general comprehensive high school.

Well, I received this new student in my class and she hadn't been successful and was behind on the credits she needed for graduation. Her name was Mary. As I began to work with her I became aware that her academic skills were very low. She had a lot of trouble communicating verbally and couldn't write effectively at all. After a while, I began to doubt if she'd ever develop the skills she needed to graduate from high school. Nevertheless, I worked with her almost constantly for that year. I saw little or no improvement.

During the last couple of weeks of school she asked me if she could be my teaching assistant (TA) for the next school year. I was shocked at this request. It was my policy to have very few TA's and the ones that I did have had to be academically sharp and highly motivated to help me with my classes. She didn't seem to have either of these requirements. It was really all I could do to control my reaction to laugh. But something inside my brain told me to rethink. My thought was, *Why not! Give it a chance! Maybe, just maybe, it might work out. Nothing that had been attempted this year had seemed to help.* So I said to Mary, "Sure, we can do that! You know that you'll have to work hard. You won't only have to do your work, but you have to help me with classroom duties as well as assist other students." She agreed.

Soon the new school year started and Mary began to work as my TA. I'd like to tell you that everything changed and that Mary became a model student and made up all her missing credits. Well, the year didn't start that way. It was more like business as usual with Mary. But we did begin to talk a great deal more.

It was my custom for TA's to sit at an extra desk that I had placed beside my own. This allowed us to have more conversations about school progress or lack of it. It also allowed us to have conversations of personal importance. Mary told me about problems and issues that she was working through and those she had already dealt with. Some of these were successful and some had bad resolutions.

Mary wasn't doing well. She seemed to be spiraling down. She began to dress in a more bizarre fashion. She started to hang around with students who were also making very bad decisions. They were congregating across the street from the school and smoking cigarettes and taking illegal drugs. Mary started to date a male student who was really out of control.

I watched this go on for a few weeks and even talked to Mary about her behavior but nothing changed! Mary and I continued to talk about a lot of different things and we really started to develop a trusting relationship.

Finally, I couldn't take it any longer. I was fed up with watching her continue her destructive behavior. She was throwing away all of the help and support she was receiving from her foster home and school.

One day I asked her to stay after class because I wanted to talk with her. I turned to Mary and told her what she could and couldn't do in her life. I told her she needed to dress in a normal fashion, no more weird clothes! I told her that she could no longer go across the street to smoke and hang out with the students who weren't taking school seriously. I also told her that she had to drop the loser she was dating! He had the reputation of being a drug dealer and she had to stay away.

I told her she needed new friends. She could only hang out with those students who were taking school seriously and working to get their credits. She needed to start taking school seriously and work as hard as she could to get all of her units and make up her missing credits as quickly as possible so she could graduate from high school! She had to do this! There were no options! She didn't say a word, but just left the room.

After she left the room I began to think about our conversation. I thought, *Was I too harsh with her? Should I have been so frank about her actions? What would our relationship be in class now?*

I left my room and walked toward the office to get some work done. As I crossed the campus Mary was standing in my path talking to her friends who she had been meeting with across the street.

As I approached, I heard her say the following. "I can't go across the street with you guys anymore. I'm going to change my dress and I'm not going to date George anymore." "Why?" came the response from her group. "Because Dr. Kirk said that I have to!" "He can't tell you to do that!" they responded. "He can't tell you what to do!" I slowed my pace so that I could hear as much as I could of the conversation. Mary said, "He told me that I had to stop all of this and I have to do it!"

I couldn't believe my ears! Wow! What emotions, thoughts and feelings went through my brain. *Could this be a turning point for Mary?* Well, it was! Mary was never the same. She began to take her schoolwork more seriously. She worked very hard to make up her credits. She changed her dress and developed new friendships! Her academic skills improved dramatically! She eventually completed her credits and graduated.

So what happened with Mary? I believe it's an example of the power or influence teachers have with their students. Yet, not just teachers. All of us have great influence over someone. It could be a child, a grandchild, someone at church or just a friend. We have the ability to greatly influence the lives of those around us for good or evil. It's a power that we need to take very seriously and utilize to help and not harm.

The truth is that all responsible caring people have this power to influence and help others. First, the relationship needs to be established with the individual that's in need of help, and then within that trusted relationship the power to influence can be exercised. People want to be successful and when a responsible, trusted person offers help they will have a chance at that success.

STEP 39: CHOICES – LAZINESS

Laziness is an easily learned behavioral trait. Its opposite, industriousness, is also a learned trait but it's more difficult to learn. Proverbs has much to say about laziness.

> *A little extra sleep, a little more slumber, and little folding of the hands to rest – and poverty will pounce on you like a bandit; scarcity will attack you like an armed robber.* Ch6 v10

> *If you love sleep, you will end in poverty. Keep your eyes open, and there will be plenty to eat!* Ch20 v13

The lazy person, whether young or old, will have a superabundance of excuses for failing to work hard or complete a job. Proverbs gives us a glimpse of these silly responses:

> *The lazy person is full of excuses, saying, "If I go outside, I might meet a lion in the streets and be killed!"* Ch22 v13

Initially, this verse brings a short laugh. How could anyone be so lazy and come up with such a ridiculous excuse? Still as a public school teacher, I heard numerous reasons or excuses why homework wasn't completed, a child was late to school, or why a project wasn't finished on time. I remembered this Proverbs example and just smiled. Remember again, any excuse is a good excuse. Still, it doesn't change the reality of the situation or the expectation of the consequences.

Proverbs tells us that there's a time of opportunity for work and if one takes that opportunity there will be rewards. The opposite is also true.

A wise youth works hard all summer; a youth who sleeps away the hour of opportunity brings shame. Ch10 v5

The summer before my senior year in high school, and for the next several summers, I worked to earn money for college. I had several jobs, and most of these jobs involved long hours and hard physical work. Unloading a railroad boxcar full of one hundred pound sacks of sugar and flour in the Oklahoma summer heat was hard physical work!

I learned many valuable lessons during these years. One lesson was that hard works pays off. I was able to save most of the money I made during those summers to pay a large part of my university expenses. Because I worked so hard for the funds needed to go to school, when the time came to go to class or to study, that's what I did. I never suffered from the need to waste any of my hard-earned money by skipping a class or not studying.

During those years I remembered the following verse in Proverbs and have never forgotten its true meaning.

Lazy people are a pain to their employer. They are like smoke in the eyes or vinegar that sets the teeth on edge. Ch10 v26

I witnessed lazy people during those years and how they chose to work harder at not working than just getting the job done. Our boss didn't care for them and they were a pain for him to deal with. I saw that the lazy workers either lost their jobs or were never given more responsibilities or greater opportunities.

Some people are so lazy that they won't even lift a finger to feed themselves. Ch19 v24

This is hard to believe especially in our modern society. Yet, our federal government has done a great job of providing incentives for people to choose not to work. They provide just enough financial assistance for individuals to get by, but little incentive for them to be vocationally trained and assisted to get a job and provide for their needs independently.

It's vital that parents teach their children to choose to be hardworking, responsible individuals that take every opportunity to enhance their lives and build a better future. Remember those doors of opportunity. Proverb's plan also tells us that it's through hard work that we become prosperous and that if we waste our time and miss out on opportunities to improve ourselves, we'll be the ones to lose out and we'll gain the title of a fool.

Hard work means prosperity; only fools idle away their time. Ch12 v11

Work hard and become a leader; be lazy and become a slave. Ch12 v24

We don't like to talk about the idea of becoming a slave in today's society. We like to think we're better and that the old idea of slavery is behind us. The fact is this is far from being the truth because there are many types of slavery. Maybe the buying and selling of human beings is mostly behind us, at least in some parts of the world, but living a life of financial slavery is real and is present in our society.

While an individual is moving through their teen years and into their twenties, there are opportunities for working hard in small but meaningful jobs, going to school and learning about themselves and the world. They have the opportunity of choosing to develop intellectual tools that will help them gain employment and secure a good paying job. This in turn leads to more opportunities and continued success. If individuals choose not to take advantage of these opportunities, these open doors can close and cost them for the rest of their lives. One only has to refer to the difference in life long earning potentials between a high school dropout, high school graduate, one with some college and one who has completed college. All things being equal the average earnings difference is stunning. The life long earnings difference between lower education and higher education levels involves hundreds of thousands of dollars.

Some may choose to make up for this difference by borrowing money. It's a mistake to try and improve ones income by borrowing money or utilizing credit cards. This begins a downward spiral of economic slavery that results in spending more and more on high interest payments on the borrowed money. This is a common modern financial trap and is one that Proverbs warns about. A wise person will choose to work hard and take advantage of opportunities to improve themselves and to establish a solid financial base.

> *Just as the rich rule the poor, so the borrower is servant to the lender.* Ch22 v7

Step 40: Choices – Don't Talk Too Much

Proverbs is clear about the value of speech and the trouble it can cause. It's certainly a valuable tool to communicate with each other or to help each other, but it can be a double-edged sword.

> *Everyone enjoys a fitting reply; it is wonderful to say the right thing at the right time!* Ch15 v23

> *Words satisfy the soul as food satisfies the stomach; the right words on a person's lips bring satisfaction.* Ch18 v20

We've all been encouraged by kind and thoughtful words of another person. It's refreshing and helpful to be uplifted by their words. Having said that, we have all been hurt by words from those who are unthinking, uncaring, hateful or careless. Perhaps the last point, careless, is the most common and dangerous misuse of speech. Carelessness, mixed with the natural tendency that many of us seem to have of talking too much, is a major hazard of communication. Whatever the case, we're warned in Proverbs that we run a risk of trouble if we talk too much.

> *If you keep your mouth shut, you will stay out of trouble.* Ch21 v23

> *Even fools are thought to be wise when they keep silent; when they keep their mouths shut, they seem intelligent.* Ch17 v28

> *Don't talk too much, for it fosters sin. Be sensible and turn off the flow!* Ch10 v1

Choosing to talk too much is a common problem for a lot of us. We feel a need to get our two cents worth into the conversation or to set others straight. We like to let others hear our point of view even if it's not requested. Most of us know that we have been blessed with the God given ability to solve other people's problems. We think all we need to do is to tell them the solution to their problems and everything will be all right. The solution to their problems is clear to us.

We like to use words to influence others to get our own way. We like to bring others around to our point of view. Sometimes we take things too far and cause hostile feelings in others.

> *Avoiding a fight is a mark of honor; only fools insist on quarreling.* Ch20 v3

> *A truly wise person uses few words; a person with understanding is even tempered.* Ch17 v27

If we choose to be wise we need to understand the power of speech. We need to try to limit the number of our words. Words have the power to hurt or to heal. A truly wise person will use fewer words in their conversations and try to use words of comfort and support for people who are in need.

Kind words are like honey — sweet to the soul and healthy for the body. Ch16 v24

Some people make cutting remarks, but the words of the wise bring healing. Ch12 v8

Those who love to talk will experience the consequences, for the tongue can kill or nourish life. Ch18 v21

Another important concept that's brought out in Proverb's plan is that what we say to others, and how we say it, can have a healthy effect on them and on us. In this day and age in which we are so health conscious, and want to live a long healthy life, it's important to understand the wisdom expressed by this plan.

Gentle words bring life and health; a deceitful tongue crushes the spirit. Ch15 v4

A person's words can be life-giving water; words of true wisdom are as refreshing as a bubbling brook. Ch18 v4

Those who control their tongue will have a long life; a quick retort can ruin everything. Ch13 v3

We've all been in situations where we were upset, our temperature began to rise, and we felt like we would explode if we didn't get our thoughts out and challenge the views before us. Too often it's during these times that we say things that we live to regret.

As we think about what we said, we begin to experience remorse. Guilt begins to fill our thoughts and we wish we could take back our words. We suffer because we want to be better. We suffer not only in our waking hours but also as we try to sleep. We wake up the next day tired and drained from our thoughtless speech. It's a hard thing to do but we can choose to control our speech and try to be helpful and uplifting to others in the things we say.

A fool gives full vent to anger, but a wise person quietly holds it back. Ch29 v11

There is more help for a fool than for someone who speaks without thinking. Ch29 v20

The godly speak words that are helpful, but the wicked speak only what is corrupt. Ch10 v32

Choosing to control the tongue is hard. It's a sign of real maturity when one finally arrives at a position in life when the tongue is mastered.

Wise speech is rarer and more valuable than gold and rubies. Ch20 v15

We need to remember that words spoken are like bullets fired from a gun. Once bullets leave the barrel they can't be recalled. Words are the same. Once foolish or destructive words are shot from our lips their effects will be made. Too many times the damage done is devastating.

STEP 41: CHOICES – HARSH WORDS

A gentle answer turns away wrath, but harsh words stir up anger. Ch15 v1

Gentle words bring life and health; a deceitful tongue crushes the spirit. Ch15 v4 *Patience can persuade a prince, and soft speech can crush strong opposition.* Ch25 v15

As we mature we should be gaining in wisdom and begin tempering the things we say in response to getting angry. To choose not to respond emotionally to angry situations with harsh words is not automatic. It's a real sign of maturity for a person to choose to control their tongue and keep their words calm and respectful in these situations.

It's good to remember when one speaks and the words are allowed to fly into the universe, those words can never be taken back. It's so very important for adults and children to remember this and to choose to think before something is said. Husbands and wives can hurt one another and their children by harsh or angry words. Those words can never be taken back. They may be forgiven but their effects will always remain. They may be less hurtful over time, but they're never really forgotten. We've all had experiences when we were called some name or talked to in such a way that we were hurt psychologically and emotionally. It ruined our day!

So, as stated in these words from Proverbs, wisdom requires us to take stock of what we're going to say before we say it. We must consider the impact that our words will have on others. Maybe we want to hurt them, but Proverbs reminds us that isn't really the wise course of action. It's hard and it takes a great deal of maturity to choose to control ones words, but it's worth the effort and will give a positive result as we grow toward gaining wisdom.

STEP 42: CHOICES – ANGER

Anger is a problem that at one time or another affects all of us. When one is very young and becomes angry it's not uncommon for outbursts to be exhibited. However, this behavior needs to be corrected very quickly by parents. Proper behaviors must be taught and reinforced by parents so children can choose appropriate ways to express their anger and discontent. If this isn't done properly, the child may believe that it's acceptable to disrupt others' lives with outbursts of anger just because they're upset. This isn't acceptable.

One can become angry and that's okay, but it isn't okay for that anger to spill over and negatively impact the lives of innocent individuals. There are many strategies that can be chosen to help deal with anger, not the least of these is to teach the child to communicate it in a proper manner. Parents can teach the child to put the situation on hold until they settle down, ask for adult assistance, or even just walk away and work on a proper response later. Children need instruction in choosing to control and deal with their anger.

Those who control their anger have great understanding;
those with a hasty temper will make many mistakes. Ch14 v29

A relaxed attitude lengthens life; ... Ch14 v30a

We know that it isn't healthy for an individual to constantly be uptight and angry. Proverbs is warning us that the probabilities of living a long, good life depend at least in some measure on our ability to handle anger. If we choose the proper behavior techniques to deal with it, the probability of living a healthier life improves. A verse in Ephesians can certainly be included in Proverb's plan:

...don't let the sun go down while you are still angry.
Ephesians 4: 26

This is very good advice. As stated earlier, when we choose to let anger get a foothold in our lives, stay upset throughout the night and into the next day, not only will we be tired from not getting a good night's rest but it sets us up for a bad day. If each day's anger is settled before bedtime, one will usually get a better night's sleep and awake more refreshed in the morning.

Many times my wife and I have spent the night talking into the wee hours of the morning working out our problems. At the time, we both wanted to just try and get some sleep; but, we chose to keep at it until we successfully talked it through. The next day we were always glad that the problems had been resolved the night before even at the cost of compromised sleep. We looked forward to a new day of communication, peace and love.

STEP 43: CHOICES – PERVERSE TALK

> *Avoid all perverse talk; stay far from corrupt speech.*
> Ch4 v24

Nothing tells us more about a person than his or her speech. I've listened to many people talk over the years in everyday conversations as well as formal speakers presenting ideas to a group. The ideas that are presented are important, but so are the words that are chosen to make their points. If profane language is chosen it'll be rejected by some of the listeners and the points that the speaker is trying to make will be lost. If the speaker uses improper pronunciation or incorrect grammar then the speaker's points will also be lost.

Speech, more than any other means of communication, tells about our heart. It's through speech that people really learn who we are and what we believe about the world. It reflects our soul, what's at the core of our beliefs and what the character of our being really is. If our speech is perverse and corrupt then so is our soul.

Proverbs isn't the only book of the Bible that warns about our speech and how our tongue can get us in trouble.

> *And the tongue is a flame of fire. It is full of wickedness*
> *that can ruin your whole life. It can turn the entire course*
> *of your life into a blazing flame of destruction, for it is set*
> *on fire by hell itself.* James 3: 6

The Bible warns us that careless, thoughtless speech is like a match that begins a raging forest fire. To be wise, it's imperative that we choose to control and guard our tongue and speech.

The temptation will always be there to give a sharp response or shape a verbal attack, to give verbally as good as we got. Yet this is dangerous and Proverbs, as well as other sections of the Bible, warn against it.

> *...but no one can tame the tongue. It is an uncontrollable evil, full of deadly poison. Sometimes it praises our Lord and Father, and sometimes it breaks into curses against those who have been made in the image of God.* James 3: 8b-9

> *We all make many mistakes, but those who control their tongues can also control themselves in every other way.* James 3: 2

The wise and the spiritually mature must choose to do better. Words can have harmful effects on others and their effects are lasting. I have said this before, once words are spoken their effects are permanent. The damage has been done and it can't be reversed. Sure, efforts for forgiveness and healing can be attempted and can be successful to some extent. However, the relationship will never be the same again and the hurt that has been caused can never be fully or completely repaired.

That's the bad news but here's the good news. Words can also heal, refresh and sustain others. They can heal as surely as many medications. We all need to choose to use words to their best advantage, to help others and to uplift. As surely as a medical doctor has power to heal those with physical disease we have the power to heal those who are hurting from the shocks and trauma of everyday living. Words can heal and help or they can harm and destroy. It's within our power to choose to help or to harm those with whom we come in contact each and every day.

It certainly isn't easy to take the high road, to return a kind word when we're verbally attacked. In fact, it's normal and easier to turn our verbal guns on those who attack us. Nevertheless, the wise and mature are able to do better. For them, people come first. They have learned to return love and forgiveness in a meaningful verbal way that helps, heals, and refreshes.

STEP 44: CHOICES – HELPING THE POOR

There can be little doubt that part of a Christian's responsibility is to help care for the poor. That can take many forms and each person will need to make choices on how to best help. It's clear throughout the Bible that we have a responsibility to help those who have fallen on hard times.

Each person who is having a hard time is still responsible to work as best as they can to make life better for themselves and their family. Some have circumstances in their lives where, for whatever reason, they have limited choices. Some of these circumstances are of their own making. However, each and every one of us is to work with what we have to improve our lives. We aren't just to stop and give up and expect others to take care of us. The Bible tells us that if a person won't work, when they are able, then they should not eat.

> *Whoever does not work should not eat.*
> 2 Thessalonians 3:10

If a person is down and needs help and can't make it with their own efforts, then it's a Christian's responsibility to help that person in every moral way possible to get back on their feet and become autonomous. Yet, it's the individual's responsibility to choose to move back to providing for themselves and their families as quickly as possible.

There's no moral authority that gives any person the right to take help from others without first doing everything legally and morally possible to work hard to stand on their own two feet. Still, there are some who are so severely injured, ill or mentally impaired that they will require constant care and help. These are few in number compared to those who need temporary assistance to get back on their feet.

Helping the poor and those who are hungry is truly a Christian responsibility. I think many of us look for little ways to help others as we move through life. Sometimes people are moved to help a homeless person standing on a busy street corner. Another time they may decide to participate in gathering food for the needy during the Thanksgiving or Christmas Seasons. There are many other legitimate ways that people can help those who are in need of food, clothing or even medical care.

> *Those who oppress the poor insult their Maker, but those who help the poor honor him.* Ch4 v31

> *Those who shut their ears to the cries of the poor will be ignored in their own time of need.* Ch21 v13

> *Blessed are those who are generous, because they feed the poor.* Ch22 v9

> *If your enemies are hungry, give them food to eat. If they are thirsty, give them water to drink. You will heap burning coals on their heads, and the Lord will reward you.* Ch25 v21-22

Helping the Poor

Tom, a friend, was impressed by God to start a food room program at his church. The idea stuck in his mind and he talked about it to his wife. Over the next several weeks they prayed about the possibility. The idea of a food room grew and became more powerful. Tom decided that he would take it to the church leadership for discussion. He made an appointment with the senior pastor and told him that God had laid the idea of a church food room on his heart. The pastor was not too sure about the idea. They had no facilities to house such a program and there was certainly not extra money in the church budget to fund such a program. Yet, the pastor decided to pray about the idea himself and told my friend that he would get back to him.

Well, time went by and nothing was decided. Tom talked to the pastor again and asked where he was in the situation. The pastor agreed that it was time to either make a move in the direction of the food room or to forget the idea. Plans were made for the pastor and my friend to meet with the church elders to discuss the matter. A meeting was called and they went before the elders with the idea and a plan to make it happen.

Part of the plan was for some of the elders to go with him to a local church food room in a nearby town. Tom had already contacted the food room and made plans to go visit. During the visit he picked the brain of the director of the program and requested any and all paperwork that they used to run the program. The director was very helpful and provided all of the needed information. Tom rapidly learned the process that was used and took this information and developed a plan for its implementation.

Armed with the plan and an invitation to come back to the food room Tom was ready for the meeting. After hearing Tom's plan and invitation to visit the food room, and his deep commitment, the elders were in agreement that the proposal needed to move forward. They made it clear that it would be Tom's task to make it a reality.

The elders, and church staff wouldn't take on the project. It would be up to Tom and his wife to organize and set up a successful program.

One bit of information was uncovered a small sum of money had been donated by a church member for use in a possible local mission project. It was proposed that this money could be used to rent or purchase a mobile building to be used by the new food room. The elders and pastor agreed that this would be a perfect use of the funds. So the green light was given for the establishment of a church food room and to use the donated funds to secure a small building.

The planning was finalized and placed into operation. A refurbished mobile school classroom was purchased and placed on the southern section of the church grounds next to the parking lot.

Volunteers were requested to come and be trained in how to work in the food room filling sacks of food and keeping the needed records on each family.

The greatest miracle of the whole process was the number and quality of the volunteers that came to serve. From the very beginning these volunteers took control of all the needed activities. They were hard workers and totally committed to the new program. They were faithful every day that the food room was scheduled to be open. There wasn't a time when the workers didn't show up to work.

Not long after the new food room was set up and in operation the economy went south. This was a national tragedy but it was especially felt in the community of the new food room. Hundreds of people began coming for food assistance. It was clear that God not only blessed this project but that he timed its beginning operation perfectly.

This food room has been in operation now for over seven years. Financial donations come in every month to purchase the needed food. There has always been enough food for the guests. No one has ever been turned away without food. During this seven-year period 25,000 people have been served. God has truly blessed the food room, its volunteers, and those who have been served. God is given the credit for this whole endeavor. He has blessed all who have been part of it.

This story clearly shows what can be accomplished when people follow God's plan and how a small beginning can grow to provide help to thousands of needy individuals.

STEP 45: CHOICES – BEING GOOD TO OTHERS

†

Do not withhold good from those who deserve it when it's in your power to help them. If you can help your neighbor now, don't say, 'Come back tomorrow, and then I'll help you' Ch3 v27-28

Helping those who are in need is a Christian responsibility and duty. God commands each of us not to be content with accumulating blessings for just ourselves, but to share those blessings with those who are in need. Sometimes that help is a random onetime act and other times it's more of a long-term event. The point is that if God blesses you with abundance in one or more areas of your life and someone comes to you and asks for help, you should choose to help. Proverbs does say to those "who deserve it" and if "it's within your power to help." This may make it a judgment call for some requests. Just remember that God has given freely to you as you try to determine your responsibility to help others in need. God is telling us to choose to help others if it's in our power to do so.

PERSONAL STORY 6

Failing Another

I remember a time in my life when I surely failed another human being. It was many years ago and I had just separated from the Air Force. I was working very hard trying to complete my advanced degree and working full time in a teaching position. I guess I was really tired from the week's work and the extra studying for graduate school. Also, my wife and I had two young children that had us running all over the house, yard and city.

I felt that I was doing well just to get out of bed, get ready and then make it to church. I was sitting through the sermon in a kind of foggy, out of body experience mode. I was there, but I was running on empty and just sort of taking up space. My private thoughts were, *I can hardly wait until the sermon is over so our family can go home, we can put the kids down for a nap and my wife and I can get some rest ourselves.*

I remember something very important happened to me. I was sitting in the balcony section of the large church on Sunday morning. A state senator and his family were sitting a few aisles over. I thought how successful he was being so young and with such a beautiful family. Yet during the sermon something kept prompting me to go and talk with him. I just couldn't seem to shake the thought that this was something I needed to do. It was the right and important thing for me.

Soon the sermon was over and the congregation was dismissed. Still the feeling was there that I needed to go talk to his man. I looked in his direction and many people had come to talk to him and his family. *What does he need of me,* I thought. *He's very popular and doesn't need me to come and talk with him.* So, I didn't go over, my family and I left and went on our way.

During the following week, this state senator went into his bathroom and took a gun with him. His wife found him a short time later; he had taken his own life. I don't know if anything I could have said would have made a difference in the fatal outcome for this young man. Yet, I have lived with the haunting thought that I might have made a difference.

Over the years, when I have been prompted to speak to another fellow human being I have taken it very seriously. We all need to realize how important our words can be. For you see, we never know what the impact of our speech may be. For some, it may make all the difference.

STEP 46: CHOICES – LOVE

Hatred stirs up quarrels, but love covers all offenses.
Ch10 v12

Whoever pursues godliness and unfailing love will find life, godliness, and honor. Ch21 v21

Proverbs reminds us that whoever wants to be godly and have unfailing love in their homes must understand there is a pursuit involved. If you live in California, then you're familiar with the concept of pursuit. Once every week or two in California there is a police pursuit where the good guys are chasing the bad guys either in cars or on foot. It's usually covered on television and if it's a car pursuit, it's occasionally good for a couple of hours. Sometimes they're fast pursuits and other times they're slow pursuits. At the end of the chase, the police usually block the car or use tack strips to blow out the tires. The car is stopped and the perpetrator, or "perp" as we call them here in California, is taken into custody.

The point I want to make is that if you desire love, just like when the police desire to catch the bad guys, there's going to be work involved. It's hard work running after someone or something. I noticed that no matter if it's a foot pursuit or a vehicle pursuit when the cops get their hands on the perp the cops are breathing hard. The adrenaline is flowing, fine motor skills are all but gone and they are fully involved in getting the arrest done. Well, that's the way we must choose to pursue love within our lives and families. We must work at it. It'll take time and energy. This may not be at the same intensity of a foot race, but it's certainly going to take effort.

We should choose to make every effort to develop the loving relationships that we desire. Whether it's with our spouse, sons or daughters, parents, brothers, sisters or friends it'll demand that we put some effort into building the loving relationship. We can certainly do little things like celebrating their birthdays, anniversaries, or graduations. Yet, most important is that we choose to share our lives with them. We must spend time with them and invest our lives in theirs and let them invest their lives in ours.

Remember during all of this pursuit, we don't have to be perfect. We'll make many mistakes. When you make a mistake in the building of the relationship remember *Unfailing love and faithfulness cover sin...* Ch16 v6a

Most people will understand that as you are working to build a loving relationship with them you'll make mistakes. Nevertheless, remember a person who is truly sorry for a bad behavior will stop it! This isn't a license to continue to hurt each other. Love will cover your sin. Just ask for forgiveness and choose to do the best job you can at building the relationship.

Work hard at choosing to build love into relationships. This will require wisdom on your part. Behave in positive ways that are seen as loving and helping. Choose to do this with care and loving concern and don't bring unnecessary trouble into your relationships. However, if you do bring trouble, you'll be the one to suffer.

> *Those who bring trouble on their families inherit only the wind.* Ch11 v29

Sometimes this requires that we choose to be the mature one and overlook the faults of others. We all know that God has given us the unique ability to see the faults in others and to know how to solve their problems. If only they would listen to us! We need to get over the temptation of pride and choose to understand this point:

> *Disregarding another person's faults preserves love; telling about them separates close friends.* Ch17 v9

We should choose to use care when we respond to our loved ones. We need to answer in a gentle way and not use harsh words to respond back in conversations, even if the other person is angry and lashing out.

Choosing a soft, gentle, and proper response is much better than angry words that are only designed to hurt.

One thing about words and it's of supreme importance to remember, and I have said it before, they can never be taken back. Again, they are like the bullet coming out of a barrel; once it's on its way it can never be retrieved until after the damage is done. Whatever the effects, they are forever. Harsh and foolish words, like a careless bullet, can do much harm. They can damage relationships for years to come. Choose to take care with your words just like you would take care with a firearm. Make sure your words go where you want them to go and that they will have a positive impact on others and not cause harm.

A bowl of soup with someone you love is better than steak with someone you hate. Ch15 v17

A gentle answer turns away wrath, but harsh words stir up anger. Ch15 v1.

Step 47: Choices – Becoming Prosperous

Good planning and hard work lead to prosperity, but hasty shortcuts lead to poverty. Ch21 v5

Those who love pleasure become poor; wine and luxury are not the way to riches. Ch21 v17

The wise have health and luxury, but fools spend whatever they get. Ch21 v20

This part of Proverb's plan informs us how to be successful and prosperous in life. These aren't really big secrets, just a clear view of reality. First to be a success, a person must choose to develop a plan for their life and to work hard. There are no shortcuts in this approach. It's planning and hard work! This will go against the grain of those who want to get rich quick. Proverbs tells us that there is no quick path to prosperity.

Purchasing lottery tickets or betting on the horses may be a dream for many, but that's all it is. Just a dream! These methods are unrealistic and unreliable. The only sure way of obtaining financial wealth and success is to choose to plan and work hard. This isn't to say that we can't learn from financial strategies and tips, because we can. There are some very good books that can give us sound financial advice.

One important piece of advice in Proverbs and in every serious financial planning book is that we should never get into a habit of spending more than we earn. We need to choose to spend less than we bring in each month and put the rest into savings both for emergencies and long-range expenses. This involves so much common sense but it seems to be so difficult. It seems so hard for individuals, cities, states and even nations. This explains a lot about states and our national debts. When an entity spends $1.10 for every $1.00 that is brought in from revenue, there will be long-term problems and consequences. It's foolish to do so.

The way to financial health is not by pursuing pleasure. Wine and luxury aren't the roads to economic health. The line between wealth and being broke is a thin one. Financial health is gained by choosing to be disciplined in spending and faithfulness in savings and investments. It's easy to waste extra money each month on excessive pleasure and lose the chance to make our savings grow into a comfortable reserve that can be used for education, emergencies and retirement. Choosing financial discipline, not the pursuit of wine or luxury, is needed to build a strong financial future.

STEP 48: CHOICES – HAUGHTINESS

Haughtiness goes before destruction; humility precedes honor. Ch18 v12

It's natural for humans to become overly impressed with themselves. As we have successful experiences in our lives it's easy to become a little prideful in our accomplishments. Life has a way of correcting this fault in most of us. There will be experiences that call our pride into question. This should be enough to keep us on the humble side of life, but we have met people, who despite these natural corrective experiences became haughty and proud. Proverbs tells us that he/she is in for a correction, one that will be painful and humbling. The plan is clear that it's better to choose to be humble and allow honor to come our way naturally than to be haughty and proud and suffer the consequences.

STEP 49: CHOICES – A WIFE

Who can find a virtuous and capable wife? She is worth more than precious rubies. Her husband can trust her, and she will greatly enrich his life. She will not hinder him but help him all her life. Ch31 v10-12

I love this verse. One of the reasons is that it's so very true. The other reason is that I have found it valid in my life with my wife. We have been married for over forty-five years and my wife is not only my best friend, a person that I can trust, but she has greatly enriched my life. She hasn't hindered me in life but has encouraged and strengthened me in everything I've done. When it's all boiled down, it's really all about a marriage relationship where there is trust, love, and support. Proverbs really got this one right.

Proverb's plan does give a warning concerning what life will be like if there's strife in the home. Care must be taken to choose to avoid strife in marriage and to deal with it quickly if it arrives.

It is better to live alone in the corner of an attic than with a contentious wife in a lovely home. Ch25 v24

Step 50: Choices – The Glory of Our Youth

✝

The glory of the young is their strength; the gray hair of experience is the splendor of the old. Ch20 v29

The glory of the young is their strength, endurance, flexibility, speed, and other characteristics that have long since left me. I can remember working on the dock loading trucks and unloading train boxcars in Oklahoma. We would load cases of canned food that weighed between thirty-five and fifty pounds onto trucks. We would also unload the boxcars that were filled with one hundred pound sacks of flour and sugar. It was hot and humid and the workday would last for up to ten hours. At the end of the day I was so tired that I couldn't even eat dinner; I just fell into bed and slept until it was time to go back to work.

I learned a lot from those work experiences. I learned the young are strong but I also learned that as we age we begin to lose that strength. I saw men who were in their forties and fifties that had aged many years physically beyond their chronological age. They had worked so hard over the years they were just about spent. They had no choice; they had to work hard to provide for their families. I learned the ability to work and work hard can be a good thing but the body will eventually wear out. It's important to choose to pace how we work and what we do to make a living so that our strength isn't gone before we've provided for our family's future. Our physical strength will be gone one day and we need to plan for that day. We need to work to grow in wisdom as our physical strength wanes. It's wise to choose to replace our lost physical strength with the strength of character and wisdom.

STEP 51: CHOICES – WORKING WITH THE UNRELIABLE

Putting confidence in an unreliable person is like chewing with a toothache or walking on a broken foot.
Ch25 v19

Time and time again companies report on what they look for in a good employee and reliability is always at the top of the list. Over the years I have talked with small business owners. I asked them what characteristics they'd like to see in young workers. They wanted their employees to be at work on time, come every scheduled workday, do the work assigned and be honest in their dealings with the business and its customers. In other words they wanted their employees to be reliable.

Being successful in life isn't about being the smartest person in the room, being the best looking, or even being the most competent. It's about choosing to be there, working hard and being honest in all interactions. There will always be a place in the workforce for a person with these characteristics.

STEP 52: CHOICES – BRAGGING

Don't brag about tomorrow, since you don't know what the day will bring. Ch27 v1

There is a story in the Bible concerning a rich, young ruler. God blessed him with large crops and barns overflowing with grain. His response was to only think about himself and a life of ease. He chose to build newer, larger barns and fill them with his new crops. His problem was that he forgot who had blessed him and who ultimately held his future. His overly self-reliant and selfish attitude wasn't received well by God. You remember how this story ended; God required his soul from him that same day. (Luke 12: 19-21)

One of the main points in this story is that we don't have a clue about what's going to happen in our future. It's in God's hands and we need to remember that whatever we have, he provided. There's a joint responsibility here. We're to work and make good choices on how to best provide for our families and ourselves. Having said that, we need to be very sure that we remember it all comes from the hand of God and we need to give him thanks. It's a partnership, with God being the major partner.

Don't praise yourself; let others do it! Ch27 v2

None of us like to be around someone who is always talking about himself. The stories always begin with "I" and go on and on. After a while, we just tune out and try to find a reason to move on. It's okay to think about yourself in a positive light, I think that's really a healthy thing. It's also okay to be successful in the activities of life. In conversation just give the other person a chance to tell about their life. In fact, ask them about their life. That's one of the best ways to keep your own conversation in check. Maybe it's a small thing, but it can make a big difference in your success in meeting and getting to know people. It will be huge in the building of good, long lasting relationships.

STEP 53: CHOICES – GOING TO WAR

No normal, sane person likes the thought of going to war. War is an awful thing and the pain and suffering that it inflicts on all involved can be staggering. We all have dreamed of a world where we can live in peace and harmony. However, General Douglas MacArthur more accurately expressed the human reality of war when he said,

"Only the dead have seen the end of war."

We've had wars throughout human history, we're involved in them all over the world today and we'll be involved in them in the future. It's part of us, as if it were in our DNA. We want what we can't have, we want to keep what we have and we want others to leave what we have alone. In short, we want the world our way and when this view is played out by all humanity there's going to be conflicts that result in wars.

What's stated in Proverb's plan is that when the possibility of war presents itself, we need to be calm and rational, putting events on hold and bring in wise advisors to discuss the situation and possible courses of action.

Going to war is usually one of the first gut reactions on being threatened by or confronted by another nation. Wise men who have been there know the sacrifice involved in war will have a perspective that's invaluable. Diplomacy and negotiations should be chosen before any final decision is made to go to war. It's always worth the discussion and effort to try to stay away from war. However, there can't be peace at any price.

History is full of examples where the desire for peace took the world into wars that were devastating. Appeasement isn't the answer. Freedom and liberty are going to be threatened; there are those who would like to see them gone. Their particular world-views won't or can't tolerate freedom and liberty. So there will be times the price of liberty and freedom will involve going to war.

Advisors must also be used to assist in the proper engagement of the war. Under our system, politicians have to make the final call on going to war, but the day to day operation of that war should come from those with the military training and experience to make wise and informed decisions. So counselors and advisors are needed to help guide the ruler in a decision to go to war and how best to wage the war to a successful end.

So don't go to war without wise guidance; victory depends on having many counselors. Ch24 v6

The horses are prepared for battle, but the victory belongs to the Lord. Ch21 v31

PERSONAL STORY 7

Vietnam Veterans

I spent a year in Vietnam flying the F-4D aircraft. Like most veterans who spent time there I saw a lot of things that were difficult to work through or try to understand. I had a strong Christian background with loving parents that saw to it that I went to church and learned the Bible. They taught me faith, hope, love and redemption and how to assimilate Christian beliefs into my life. Even with this background the Vietnam experience was a tough go. Yet, by God's grace, I moved through it, returned home and separated from the Air Force.

After my service in the Air Force, I went back to school to finish my college degrees. While there I became friends with several veterans who had also spent time in combat in Vietnam. It was evident in many of their facial expressions, composure and actions that they hadn't as yet come to grips with what had happened to them in Vietnam. Several of the men and I would pool together during social events and trade a word or two about our military experiences. Not a lot was expressed verbally but nonverbally it was clear that many of these men were suffering.

It wasn't long until some asked if they could come over to our house and spend time talking. Several of them came over unannounced. Of course our door was always open to them. A very curious situation seemed to arise on almost every visit. The men really didn't want to have a two-way dialog, they just wanted to be heard. They wanted someone to just listen to their stories along with the guilt, pain and remorse that seemed to flow from every story.

One topic was always on the top of every veteran's story. They just couldn't believe that God could forgive them for what they had done while in Southeast Asia. Most of the time they wouldn't reveal what the behavior was that was causing them so much pain and sorrow.

I tried to express to them as best I could that God is a loving God who's in the business of forgiving. Nothing we can do or have done can separate us from God's love. Most would have nothing to do with it. They were so guilt ridden from the past events in combat that they just couldn't accept the reality that they could be forgiven.

Many sat and wept. They started their stories but soon couldn't continue. I sat with them and let the powerful emotions flow over them. At the time I didn't know if it was helping these men or not. I guess I still don't know for sure but I believe that just the act of expressing their feelings in a caring atmosphere was helpful to them.

The years have come and gone and I have lost track of most of these men but I will never forget their pain, suffering, and guilt. War takes a terrible toll on those it touches. It has been said that there are no unwounded soldiers. Over the years more interaction with veterans and the experiences of life have reinforced two things to me.

One is that those who have experienced the horrors of war need special help upon their return to civilian life. The second item is that no matter what is done or not done in our lives, God stands ready and willing to forgive, heal and restore us. God's very being is one of love and his redemptive power is available to all who come to him. Proverbs is correct, the wise seek counsel before going to war but counsel is also needed after the war is over.

Step 54: Choices – Strength

If you fail under pressure, your strength is not very great. Ch24 v10

One of the big issues in guiding and building our lives through choices is that sometimes it seems like our choices are limited. The ones that appear are immersed in a sea of trouble, doubt and fear. We begin to lose strength; the longer and tougher the ordeal the more our strength wanes. This is the time when we have to double down, be strong and work hard to choose to be strong. We all have an inner strength that we haven't tapped. It's when great trouble or problems come into our lives that we're provided with a marvelous opportunity to start another search to find our inner strength.

God has promised that he'll give us the strength and support we need through any circumstance in our lives. He has unlimited strength. He provides that inner grit and stamina that can help us hunker down and let the violent storms with their dark clouds pass over us.

This inner strength that I am talking about is learned through years of struggle with smaller problems and choosing to rely on God in the small things. We begin with conquering the smaller problems of life and progress to larger ones. Over time our strength and faith grow in a partnership with God and we can conquer larger issues. Our strength, faith, and determination can be victorious through life's greatest challenges. Don't ever underestimate yourself and the God given strength that you can possess. With God's help, your strength can be great and sustained. Never, never, ever give up!

STEP 55: CHOICES – FRIENDSHIP

Never abandon a friend—either yours or your father's.
Ch27 v10

As iron sharpens iron, a friend sharpens a friend.
Ch27 v17

Friendship is a precious thing. Unfortunately, many times we don't fully appreciate friendships until we are older. What we learn through the years is that the number of real friends has dropped off to a very special few. I used to hear that if we had three to five real friends in our lifetime that we were blessed. I thought, *that's not very many people.* However, over the years I have come to realize that this is indeed true.

There are some people, who for whatever reason, just connect with your heart. You develop a deep friendship and will always be friends. It's not a matter of who you are or how much you have done for them, but through the years something just clicked and your lives joined forever. They are and will always be your friends, no matter what!

It's a very special and wonderful thing. If you have three to five people with whom you have this kind of a relationship, you are indeed a fortunate person. We all need to value friendships. We need regular contact with people who love and value us. Proverb's plan reminds us not to abandon our friends for they are of great value.

STEP 56: CHOICES – GUARDING YOUR HEART

Above all else, guard your heart, for it affects everything you do. Ch4 v23

As a face reflects in water, so the heart reflects the person. Ch27 v19

We're told over and over again in the Bible that the center of our being is our heart. Of course, the Bible isn't talking about the muscular pump of the body that sends blood throughout our organs. It's talking about our mind, our soul, and all that is involved in making us a person. It's what we really are! The brain, its thoughts, its emotions and our eternal spirit are all wrapped up into our heart. Proverb's plan warns us to guard our heart, to protect it against things that can change and harm us. We are warned that once we choose to bring something into the consciousness of our brain we'll never be the same again.

If pure and good things are brought into the reality of our thoughts, then our hearts will grow positively and we'll become wiser, more loving, and more understanding. If on the other hand evil and perverse things are brought into our mind, then these will also influence our thoughts, but with negative consequences. We're warned to be careful about the crude, perverse content that we can encounter. This includes the television shows we choose to watch, the movies we go to, the music we listen to and the conversations we have. As the body reflects choices of diet and exercise, the heart reflects ethical and moral choices.

STEP 57: CHOICES – MORAL LEADERSHIP

Without wise leadership, a nation falls; with many counselors, there is safety. Ch11 v14

When there is moral rot within a nation, its government topples easily. But with wise and knowledgeable leaders, there is stability. Ch28 v2

Fearing people is a dangerous trap, but to trust the Lord means safety. Ch29 v25

Proverb's plan does have suggestions for being a wise and ethical leader. It involves several attributes. Good moral leadership involves choosing to utilize many counselors, being wise and knowledgeable, and trust God.

It takes great courage for leaders to do the right thing. For too many leaders their job automatically becomes keeping their jobs. They want to please the boss, stay with the group, be a team player and not create controversy. Their battle cry is, *"don't rock the boat."* This isn't leadership. We need to choose to follow Proverb's plan.

STEP 58: CHOICES – HAPPINESS

The godly can look forward to happiness, while the wicked can expect only wrath. Ch11 v23

This is one of the great promises in Proverbs. There's a reward for choosing to follow God and live ones life in accordance with his word and principles. That reward is happiness. The concept of happiness isn't what one might think. It doesn't mean a constant state of bliss, always laughing, having everything that one might want or having a high paying job. What it does mean is that the Godly person can look forward to a life that's going to have the hand of God placed upon it. They won't always have everything they want but they will have what they need.

Happiness for the Christian isn't in things, status or prestige but in the calm assurance that whatever events occur in life, God will be there to assist and help no matter what. Evil people can expect just the opposite. They can expect that God won't be there in the daily events of their lives. No matter how successful they may appear, they ultimately will have a life that's filled with dismay and disappointment.

The Godly will have a peace about life that no matter what happens, they won't be alone, and that the outcome of all events will ultimately be good for them and their family.

STEP 59: CHOICES – IMMORAL WOMEN

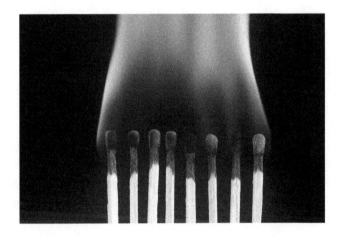

Proverbs is very clear about the dangers encountered in becoming involved in an immoral sexual relationship. It uses words like poison, death, grave, victim, ruin and poverty to describe the results of such activity. It tells of the dangers of an affair in an adulterous relationship including the warning that it may very well cost one their reputation, fortune, and even their life.

That being said, throughout history and into the modern era, men and women have chosen to have adulterous affairs that cost them dearly. Businessmen lose their fortunes, pastors lose their positions and careers while politicians have to resign from office. Homes and marriages are also torn apart from affairs. Proverb's plan is so clear about these dangers and warns over and over again of the consequences. However, it seems that the lessons are never fully learned or followed.

There are many reasons why affairs are so damaging in relationships. Not the least of these is that it often results in an attempted cover up.

All kinds of lies are told and deception runs rampant. The result is all trust and credibility disappear. What at one time was a healthy truthful relationship has now exploded and been destroyed. The word exploded is a good word to describe the results. So often lives are left in fractured pieces making it very hard to put back together. The pain for the individuals involved is immense!

Proverb's plan tells us to *rejoice in the wife of our youth*. We are to be satisfied with building a fruitful life together and to choose to be faithful in this primary of all relationships. At times it may be tempting to do otherwise. Remember evil and how active it is and what its goals are. It is to destroy your life. Proverb tells us to be wise and choose God's way. It may not be easy at times considering the temptations that are constantly being promoted on television and in the movies. These can also be found on our computers as we search the web looking for information and news. We need to choose to be wise and not play the part of a fool.

> *The lips of an immoral woman are as sweet as honey, and her mouth is smoother than oil. But the result is as bitter as poison, sharp as a double-edged sword. Her feet go down to death; her steps lead straight to the grave. For she does not care about the path to life. She staggers down a crooked trail and doesn't even realize where it leads.* Ch5 v3 -6

> *For a prostitute will bring you to poverty, and sleeping with another man's wife may cost you your very life. Can a man scoop fire into his lap and not be burned?* Ch6 v26-27

> *Follow my advice, my son; always treasure my commands. Obey them and live! Guard my teachings as your most precious possession. Tie them on your fingers as a reminder. Write them deep within your heart. Love wisdom like a sister; make insight a beloved member of your family. Let them hold you back from an affair with an immoral woman, from listening to the flattery of an adulterous woman.* Ch7 v1-5

For she has been the ruin of many; numerous men have been her victims. Her house is the road to the grave. Her bedroom is the den of death. Ch7 v26-27

A woman who is beautiful but lacks discretion is like a gold ring in a pig's snout. Ch11 v22

Let your wife be a fountain of blessing for you Rejoice in the wife of your youth... May you always be captivated by her love. Ch5 v18-19

Step 60: Choices – Summary

We are born into the world ill prepared to deal with the challenges that present themselves. We come into the world without knowledge, experience, intellectual and vital motor skills. We are totally helpless to function in a world that has inviolate physical, emotional, and spiritual laws. In all of these domains the laws offer constancy and support if they are known and followed; however, if these laws and principles are violated then the result will be pain, suffering and even death. This is as sure as the law of gravity being tested by an individual stepping off a high cliff.

There is no question about the consequences. They are predictable and consistent. This is also true of emotional and spiritual laws and their boundaries. Yet we aren't born with knowledge of these many restrictions and limitations. We know nothing of the God of the universe, or of his laws and expectations for our conduct. We are, in short, in desperate trouble and totally dependent on the care of others.

Initially this care of others is the responsibility of parents who have decided to bring life into the world. We have discussed that it's a God given responsibility for parents to train and raise children in the knowledge and understanding of the world with a reverence for God.

Children also have a responsible to listen and learn from their parents. With this joint knowledge and training children can begin to make choices that will be in concert with the laws and principles of God and nature, thereby avoiding much pain and suffering.

The child's education should include general principles on how the world operates. The laws of gravitation and physics must be explained and cautions learned to keep them safe from numerous dangerous situations. They must be taught to think, problem solve and interact with the world successfully.

Throughout life it must be emphasized that people are ultimately responsible for their choices. It's the sum total of thousands and thousands of individual choices that will determine how our lives will progress and how successful we'll become. It's not legitimate to blame others for our status in life; we are responsible. For good or for ill we hold the keys to our own success or failure. God wants to be our partner in our travels through life but once again this is our choice. We can choose to go it alone or ask the God of the universe to be our guide and help.

There are limited opportunities presented in life to build a better future. We may fail to take advantage of some of these, but if we fail to do so too often we will suffer, never reaching our full potential and even destroying our futures. We should never let a door of opportunity close.

Wisdom comes into play in all of this. It's the wise person who asks God into their life and seeks his help and direction. It's the wise who take advantage of every opportunity or open door that's set in front of them. The wise follow the boundaries and restrictions that are outlined in the laws of life. They work hard to avoid suffering needlessly because of poor choices.

So in summary, the outcome of our life is dependent on our choices, choices that are grounded in the real world and in the reality of God. The outcome of our life will depend on the quality of choices that we make. We can build a solid foundation on which to live our lives in safety and health or we can devastate our lives by making choices built on the shifting sands of relativism, foolishness and sin. We can take advantage of doors of opportunity that open before us or we can let them pass by and suffer their loss.

The really good news in all of this is God always stands ready to forgive us of our failures and careless behaviors. God's major characteristic is love and he wants to love us and help us be successful. He always stands ready to redeem us into a better existence. It is our choice.

STATEMENT OF MY FAITH CONCERNING GOD'S SALVATION MESSAGE

I have listened to many sermons delivered on the verses found in Matthew 7: 21–23. You know, the sheep and the goat one. The main point provided to those in attendance was individual salvation is a kind of guessing game. The sermons implied that on judgment day, individuals would be standing in a long line waiting to be judged. One won't have a clue on how he or she will be accepted by God. One might be expecting to hear "Well done my good and faithful servant" only to receive the bad news that God doesn't recognize him as saved and that he/she will be told to depart from God and labeled as an evildoer.

I don't believe, in the totality of the Bible message, that this is a true interpretation of these verses. Over and over again in the Bible we are told by God the Father, Jesus the son, and many apostles that this isn't how the salvation experience works. Let me give a few clear Biblical examples:

1. *For God so loved the world that he gave his only son, so that everyone who believes in him will not perish but have eternal life.* John 3: 16

2. *For if you confess with your mouth that Jesus is Lord and believe in your heart that God raised him from the dead, you will be saved. For it is by believing in your heart that you are made right with God, and it is by confessing with your mouth that you are saved.* Romans 10: 9-10

3. *God saved you by his special favor when you believed. And you can't take credit for this; it is a gift from God. Salvation is not a reward for the good things we have done, so none of us can boast about it. For we are God's masterpiece. He has created us anew in Christ Jesus, so we can do the good things he planned for us long ago.* Ephesians 2: 8–10

<u>*King James Version*</u>
For by grace are ye saved through faith; and that not of yourselves: it is the gift of God: Not of works, lest any man should boast. Ephesians 2: 8-9

4. *Your reward for trusting him will be the salvation of your souls.*1 Peter 1: 9

5. *And I am convinced that nothing can ever separate us from his love. Death can't, and life can't. The angels can't, and the demons can't. Our fears for today, our worries about tomorrow, and even the powers of hell can't keep God's love away. Whether we are high above the sky or in the deepest ocean, nothing in all creation will ever be able to separate us from the love of God that is revealed in Christ Jesus our Lord.* Romans 8: 38-39.

We are saved by our belief and faith in God's plan of Jesus dying on the cross and being raised again to pay the debt for our individual sins. That's it! We are saved by the power and blood of our savior Jesus Christ. This is no guessing game, no trick or any work we can do. We are commanded to follow God's teachings and that should reflect our desire to serve him. But he doesn't hold his teachings over our heads as a threat that somehow Jesus' work on the cross isn't enough to save us. We'll all sin after accepting Jesus as our savior and we should seek forgiveness and always work to be better followers of God's plan.

Our behavior isn't the deciding factor in our salvation. It's one thing and one thing only. That deciding factor is did we make a conscious and honest decision at one point in our lives to accept Jesus as our savior and make that decision known to God? If we did that, and were not frauds in that decision, if we came with integrity and truthfulness, our future is sealed securely in the hands of God himself. If we were frauds concerning that acceptance of God's gift of salvation through faith in Jesus then it's a different story. However, if we were truthful and honest then God will be faithful to meet us with open arms when our work on earth is done. There will be no guessing or holding our breath while waiting in line on judgment day.

REFERENCES

1. Unless otherwise indicated, all Scripture quotations are taken from the Holy Bible, New Living Translation, copyright (c) 1996, 2004, 2007, 2013 by Tyndale House Foundation. Used by Permission of Tyndale House Publishers, Inc., Carol Stream, Illinois 60188. All rights reserved.

2. Healthy lifestyles reduce the incidence of chronic disease and dementia: Evidence for the Caerphilly Cohort Study. Published December 9, 2013

3. Getty Images, Thinkstock, 2014

CPSIA information can be obtained
at www.ICGtesting.com
Printed in the USA
LVHW051358020519
616134LV00001B/2/P

9 781496 959836